Violence
OPPOSING VIEWPOINTS®

OTHER BOOKS OF RELATED INTEREST

OPPOSING VIEWPOINTS SERIES

American Values
Censorship
Civil Liberties
Culture Wars
Gangs
Hate Groups
The Information Revolution
Juvenile Crime
Mass Media
Pornography
Teens at Risk
Violence

CURRENT CONTROVERSIES SERIES

Computers and Society
Ethics
Free Speech
Hate Crimes
The Information Highway
Urban Terrorism
Violence in the Media
Youth Violence

AT ISSUE SERIES

The Media and Politics
The Future of the Internet

Media Violence

OPPOSING VIEWPOINTS®

David L. Bender, *Publisher*
Bruno Leone, *Executive Editor*
Bonnie Szumski, *Editorial Director*
Brenda Stalcup, *Managing Editor*
Scott Barbour, *Senior Editor*
William Dudley, *Book Editor*

OPPOSING
VIEWPOINTS®
SERIES

Greenhaven Press, Inc., San Diego, California

Cover photo: Annie Reesman

Library of Congress Cataloging-in-Publication Data

Media violence : opposing viewpoints / William Dudley, book editor.
    p.   cm. — (Opposing viewpoints series)
    Includes bibliographical references and index.
    ISBN 1-56510-945-7 (lib. bdg. : alk. paper). —
ISBN 1-56510-944-9 (pbk. : alk. paper)
    1. Violence in mass media. I. Dudley, William, 1964–   . II. Series:
Opposing viewpoints series (Unnumbered)
P96.V5M43 1999
303.6—dc21   98-22828
                                                                      CIP

Greenhaven Press, Inc., P.O. Box 289009
San Diego, CA 92198-9009

"CONGRESS SHALL MAKE
NO LAW...ABRIDGING THE
FREEDOM OF SPEECH, OR OF
THE PRESS."

First Amendment to the U.S. Constitution

The basic foundation of our democracy is the First
Amendment guarantee of freedom of expression. The
Opposing Viewpoints Series is dedicated to the
concept of this basic freedom and the idea that it is
more important to practice it than to enshrine it.

CONTENTS

**Chapter 3: How Should Society Respond to Media
   Violence?**

Chapter 4: Does Media Violence Have Artistic Value?

WHY CONSIDER OPPOSING VIEWPOINTS?

"The only way in which a human being can make some approach to knowing the whole of a subject is by hearing what can be said about it by persons of every variety of opinion and studying all modes in which it can be looked at by every character of mind. No wise man ever acquired his wisdom in any mode but this."

John Stuart Mill

In our media-intensive culture it is not difficult to find differing opinions. Thousands of newspapers and magazines and dozens of radio and television talk shows resound with differing points of view. The difficulty lies in deciding which opinion to agree with and which "experts" seem the most credible. The more inundated we become with differing opinions and claims, the more essential it is to hone critical reading and thinking skills to evaluate these ideas. Opposing Viewpoints books address this problem directly by presenting stimulating debates that can be used to enhance and teach these skills. The varied opinions contained in each book examine many different aspects of a single issue. While examining these conveniently edited opposing views, readers can develop critical thinking skills such as the ability to compare and contrast authors' credibility, facts, argumentation styles, use of persuasive techniques, and other stylistic tools. In short, the Opposing Viewpoints Series is an ideal way to attain the higher-level thinking and reading skills so essential in a culture of diverse and contradictory opinions.

In addition to providing a tool for critical thinking, Opposing Viewpoints books challenge readers to question their own strongly held opinions and assumptions. Most people form their opinions on the basis of upbringing, peer pressure, and personal, cultural, or professional bias. By reading carefully balanced opposing views, readers must directly confront new ideas as well as the opinions of those with whom they disagree. This is not to simplistically argue that everyone who reads opposing views will—or should—change his or her opinion. Instead, the series enhances readers' understanding of their own views by encouraging confrontation with opposing ideas. Careful examination of others' views can lead to the readers' understanding of the logical inconsistencies in their own opinions, perspective on why they hold an opinion, and the consideration of the possibility that their opinion requires further evaluation.

EVALUATING OTHER OPINIONS

To ensure that this type of examination occurs, Opposing Viewpoints books present all types of opinions. Prominent spokespeople on different sides of each issue as well as well-known professionals from many disciplines challenge the reader. An additional goal of the series is to provide a forum for other, less known, or even unpopular viewpoints. The opinion of an ordinary person who has had to make the decision to cut off life support from a terminally ill relative, for example, may be just as valuable and provide just as much insight as a medical ethicist's professional opinion. The editors have two additional purposes in including these less known views. One, the editors encourage readers to respect others' opinions—even when not enhanced by professional credibility. It is only by reading or listening to and objectively evaluating others' ideas that one can determine whether they are worthy of consideration. Two, the inclusion of such viewpoints encourages the important critical thinking skill of objectively evaluating an author's credentials and bias. This evaluation will illuminate an author's reasons for taking a particular stance on an issue and will aid in readers' evaluation of the author's ideas.

As series editors of the Opposing Viewpoints Series, it is our hope that these books will give readers a deeper understanding of the issues debated and an appreciation of the complexity of even seemingly simple issues when good and honest people disagree. This awareness is particularly important in a democratic society such as ours in which people enter into public debate to determine the common good. Those with whom one disagrees should not be regarded as enemies but rather as people whose views deserve careful examination and may shed light on one's own.

Thomas Jefferson once said that "difference of opinion leads to inquiry, and inquiry to truth." Jefferson, a broadly educated man, argued that "if a nation expects to be ignorant and free . . . it expects what never was and never will be." As individuals and as a nation, it is imperative that we consider the opinions of others and examine them with skill and discernment. The Opposing Viewpoints Series is intended to help readers achieve this goal.

David L. Bender & Bruno Leone,
Series Editors

INTRODUCTION

*"Violence in our society has reached epidemic proportions.
... Violence in the media for entertainment purposes has
been established as a major contributing factor."*
—Deborah Prothrow-Stith

*"The pathologies that affect America don't come out of a
TV tube."*
—Lionel Chetwynd

People throughout the United States were deeply shocked on
March 24, 1998, when two boys—ages thirteen and eleven—
were accused of deliberately ambushing and shooting at a
crowd of students at Westside Middle School in Jonesboro,
Arkansas. Dressed in camouflage fatigues and firing high-pow-
ered rifles, the two attackers killed four students and one
teacher. In attempting to come to terms with this tragic and baf-
fling event, Mike Huckabee, the governor of Arkansas, said, "I
don't know what else we'd expect in a culture where children
are exposed to tens of thousands of murders on television and
movies. It's a cultural disease."

Huckabee's statement is representative of a long-standing tradition of criticizing violence in the media. During the nine-
teenth century, educators and others warned about the effects of
lurid dime novels and newspaper crime stories on the young. In
the early twentieth century, motion pictures and radio were both
viewed as significant social threats. Today, concerns are expressed
about violence in computer games, popular songs, and on the
Internet. Throughout the evolving changes in media technology,
some fundamental questions have remained the same: Do depictions of violence in the media somehow contribute to real-life
violence such as the Jonesboro tragedy? Are viewers of media violence encouraged to commit violence themselves?

Since the 1950s, television has been at the center of the debate over media violence. There are several reasons for the focus
on television. It is pervasive: 98 percent of American households
have at least one television set. It is heavily watched: Studies have
estimated that children and adolescents watch television for
twenty-two to twenty-eight hours a week. Finally, television
shows are frequently violent. In one 1982 study, researchers
who analyzed 180 hours of programming counted 1,846 acts of

violence. The net result of television's popularity and violent content is that the average American child witnesses eight thousand murders and one hundred thousand other acts of violence by the time he or she finishes elementary school.

Many argue that exposure to such quantities of violent depictions damages children and contributes to violence in real life. In particular, critics claim that television violence promotes aggression, teaches children that violence is an acceptable solution to problems, and fosters a fearful attitude by leading viewers to think that the world is more violent than it really is.

Opponents of television violence cite both scientific studies and anecdotal evidence to back up their claims. Psychologists and social researchers have performed hundreds of scientific studies of the effects of television violence. Critics of television violence point to investigations such as a 1956 experiment that found that children who watched violent cartoons subsequently engaged in more disruptive and destructive behaviors than those who watched nonviolent cartoons. Another noted study tracked the lives and viewing habits of a group of children over a period of twenty-two years; it found that those who viewed the most violent television programs as children were more likely to become violent criminals or exhibit other problems as they grew into young adulthood. Leonard Eron, coauthor of this study, concluded that watching television violence was the best predictor of violent behavior later in life. "There can no longer be any doubt," he told Congress in 1992, "that heavy exposure to televised violence is one of the causes of aggressive behavior, crime and violence in society."

In addition to the scientific evidence, opponents of television violence argue that many anecdotal stories suggest a connection between media and real-life violence. A nine-year-old who shot up a building in New York City explained to a police sergeant how he learned to load his automatic weapon: "I watch a lot of TV." Mark Branch, a nineteen-year-old Massachusetts youth, stabbed to death a female college student and then killed himself; his room was found to contain ninety horror movies and the machete and goalie mask made famous by a character in the *Friday the* 13th film series. "Ask any homicide cop from London to Los Angeles to Bangkok if television violence induces real-life violence," writes journalist Carl M. Cannon, "and listen carefully to the cynical, knowing laugh."

However, other commentators question both the scientific and anecdotal evidence linking television violence with real-life violence. Children in research situations who exhibit aggressive behavior shortly after watching television do not necessarily demonstrate how television affects viewers in the real world or over a period of years, these critics contend. Others argue that finding a correlation between television violence and violent behavior does not prove that television violence *causes* such behavior. Psychology professor Kevin Durkin concludes that even if one accepts the most compelling research demonstrating a link between television violence and aggressive behavior, "the relationship between viewing and aggressive behavior is a weak one. Nobody has ever demonstrated otherwise."

Many also question the persuasiveness of anecdotal stories linking specific crimes to media depictions such as the *Friday the 13th* series. Again, a key point is that a correlation between a certain violent motion picture or television show and a particular crime does not prove that one caused the other. For example, instead of being inspired by *Friday the 13th* to commit murder, Mark Branch could have been drawn to watch the series *because* he was a violent person by nature. "I've seen *Friday the 13th* and I haven't killed anyone," writes journalist David Futrelle. "Why do we imagine that others react to images like Pavlovian dogs?" To suggest that motion pictures "induce" people like Mark Branch to commit murder, Futrelle argues, "is pushing the concept of 'anecdotal evidence' well past the breaking point."

Blaming the media for violence, some believe, diverts attention from the true roots of violence. "Anyone looking for the causes of rampant violence in American society," Futrelle asserts, "would do better to stick to a familiar list: poverty, racism, parental violence, the ready accessibility of guns." However, as historian Todd Gitlin argues, "There is little political will for a war on poverty, guns, or family breakdown." Instead, Gitlin contends, "we are offered a crusade against media violence . . . a feel-good exercise, a moral panic substituting for practicality." Gitlin and others assert that political leaders exploit public concern over media violence to avoid dealing with more pressing social problems.

Whether television violence leads people to commit violent acts is one of several controversies investigated in *Media Violence: Opposing Viewpoints*. Differing opinions on the harms of media violence and the proper societal response are examined in the following chapters: Is Violence in the Media a Serious Problem? Should the Government Restrict Media Violence? How Should Society Respond to Media Violence? Does Media Violence Have Artistic Value? The authors featured in this volume express diverse views about the morality, aesthetics, psychological effects, and social implications of violence in the media.

IS VIOLENCE IN THE MEDIA A SERIOUS PROBLEM?

CHAPTER PREFACE

In 1977, Ronny Zamora, a fifteen-year-old Costa Rican immigrant who lived in New York City with his mother and stepfather, was tried for the murder of his eighty-two-year-old neighbor. Apparently Zamora had shot the woman after she had discovered him robbing her home; he subsequently fled in the victim's car. During Zamora's trial, his lawyer offered a novel defense: He argued that Zamora should not be held responsible for his crime because he was the victim of a type of insanity that stemmed from being "under the influence of prolonged, intense, involuntary, subliminal television intoxication." Beginning when he was a young child, Zamora had spent countless hours home alone watching TV while his mother worked. Expert witnesses testified that television had given the boy distorted ideas about the nature of violence and had conditioned Zamora to react the way he did when the neighbor found him in her home. The shooting, they surmised, was a conditioned reflex based on his exposure to violent television.

Prosecutors and other expert witnesses strongly disagreed. The television shows Zamora watched, they argued, should have taught him that killing was wrong and that criminals were generally punished, not rewarded. In fact, they maintained, Zamora had evidently learned those lessons, since he had muffled the gunshot with a pillow and attempted to hide and destroy evidence after his crime. "Where have we gotten," the prosecutor asked the jury, "when someone can come into a court of law and, with a straight face, ask you to excuse the death of a human being because the killer watches television?" The jury ultimately found the defendant guilty.

The Zamora case presents an extreme example of a central question about media violence: Does it cause or contribute to violence in real life? While few would go so far as to excuse Zamora's actions, many social researchers who have studied television and media violence have concluded that it does affect children, making them more aggressive and less sensitive to the pain of others. Some long-term studies have shown a correlation between heavy television watching as a child and a greater likelihood of being arrested for criminal acts as an adult. But other researchers have questioned the validity of studies that suggest links between media violence and real-life crime. Whether media violence has serious effects on society is examined in the viewpoints in the following chapter.

| "There are substantial risks of harmful effects from viewing violence throughout the television environment."

TELEVISION VIOLENCE IS A SERIOUS PROBLEM

National Television Violence Study

The National Television Violence Study, a three-year research project begun in 1994, was funded by the National Cable Television Association and administered by Mediascope, a nonprofit media education organization. The study involved the efforts of media scholars at the University of California at Santa Barbara, the University of Texas at Austin, the University of Wisconsin at Madison, and the University of North Carolina at Chapel Hill. The following viewpoint is excerpted from the researchers' initial report, which was issued in February 1996. The study's authors conclude that not only is television violence common, but it is also frequently presented in ways that could harm viewers. For example, they argue, programs rarely show negative consequences of violence and television characters who use violence often go unpunished. Violence presented in such a context can desensitize viewers to violence and can even encourage violent behavior, the authors maintain.

As you read, consider the following questions:

1. What were the two principal goals of the National Television Violence Study?
2. On what three distinct levels was violent television content analyzed by the researchers of the NTVS?
3. According to the study, how did children respond to advisories warning about violent content in particular TV programs?

Reprinted from the National Television Violence Study, 1994–1995: Summary of Findings and Recommendations (1996) at www.igc.apc.org/mediascope/ntvssmfn.htm, by permission of Mediascope.

Violence on television may be presented in many different forms and settings. It may be performed by heroic characters or by villains. It may be rewarded, or it may be punished. Violence may occur without much victim pain and suffering, or it may cause tremendous physical anguish. It may be shown close-up on the screen or at a distance.

These and other similar variations represent the context of television violence. Such contextual features hold important implications for the influence of television violence on the audience. Some depictions of violence are likely to contribute to harmful effects on viewers, whereas other portrayals may be pro-social and beneficial for the audience.

The study has two principal goals:

- To identify the contextual features associated with violent depictions that most significantly increase the risk of a harmful effect on the audience.
- To analyze the television environment in depth to report on the nature and extent of violent depictions, focusing in particular on the relative presence of the most problematic portrayals.

THE STUDY'S FRAMEWORK

This study is the most elaborate and comprehensive scientific assessment yet conducted of the context in which violence is depicted on television. Precise quantitative content analysis techniques were employed, enabling evaluation of differences among a wide range of contextual features of violence.

The foundation for the content analysis was a review of the entire body of existing scientific knowledge regarding the impact of television violence. This analysis identified three primary types of harmful effects associated with viewing violence: learning aggressive attitudes and behaviors, becoming desensitized to real-world violence, and developing fear of being victimized by violence. The risk of such effects occurring is influenced strongly by the contextual patterns, or the ways in which violence is depicted.

In order to accurately assess the contextual elements in television content, it is necessary to consider multiple levels of analysis within each program. Some context features occur at the level of interactions between characters. Others can be understood only by considering the entire program as a whole. For example, a victim might not express pain during a violent attack but may be depicted later in the plot as suffering emotionally and financially. In other words, context factors may be revealed as a plot unfolds.

To consider these different aspects of a program, the study analyzed television content at three distinct levels: 1) how characters interact with one another when violence occurs (labeled a violent interaction), 2) how violent interactions are grouped together (labeled a violent scene), and 3) how violence is presented in the context of the overall program. Additional analyses were conducted on reality-based programs to examine the ways in which violence in non-fiction content may be discussed, reported, or talked about, as opposed to being depicted visually.

For the study, violence was defined as any overt depiction of the use of physical force—or the credible threat of such force—intended to physically harm an animate being or group of beings. Violence also includes certain depictions of physically harmful consequences against an animate being or group that occur as a result of unseen violent means.

This study is based on the largest and most representative sample of television ever examined using scientific content analysis procedures. Researchers randomly selected programs on 23 television channels over a 20-week period to create a composite week of content for each source. The study monitored programs between the hours of 6:00 A.M. and 11:00 P.M., a total of 17 hours a day across seven days of the week, yielding a sum of approximately 119 hours per channel. In total, this project examined approximately 2,500 hours of television programming that includes 2,693 programs; 384 of these were reality-based shows.

KEY FINDINGS

• *The context in which most violence is presented on television poses risks for viewers.* The majority of programs analyzed in this study contain some violence. But more important than the prevalence of violence is the contextual pattern in which most of it is shown. The risks of viewing the most common depictions of televised violence include learning to behave violently, becoming more desensitized to the harmful consequences of violence, and becoming more fearful of being attacked. The contextual patterns noted below are found consistently across most channels, program types, and times of day. Thus, there are substantial risks of harmful effects from viewing violence throughout the television environment.

• *Perpetrators go unpunished in 73% of all violent scenes.* This pattern is highly consistent across different types of programs and channels. The portrayal of rewards and punishments is probably the most important of all contextual factors for viewers as they interpret the meaning of what they see on television. When violence is presented without punishment, viewers are more likely to learn the lesson that violence is successful.

• *The negative consequences of violence are not often portrayed in violent programming.* Most violent portrayals do not show the victim experiencing any serious physical harm or pain at the time the violence occurs. For example, 47% of all violent interactions show no harm to victims, and 58% show no pain. Even less frequent is the depiction of any long-term consequences of violence. In fact, only 16% of all programs portray the long-term negative repercussions of violence, such as psychological, financial, or emotional harm.

Reprinted by permission of Kirk Anderson.

• *One out of four violent interactions on television (25%) involve the use of a handgun.* Depictions of violence with guns and other conventional weapons can instigate or trigger aggressive thoughts and behaviors.

• *Only 4% of violent programs emphasize an anti-violence theme.* Very few violent programs place emphasis on condemning the use of violence or on presenting alternatives to using violence to solve problems. This pattern is consistent across different types of programs and channels.

• *On the positive side, television violence is usually not explicit or graphic.* Most violence is presented without any close-up focus on aggressive behaviors and without showing any blood and gore. In particular, less than 3% of violent scenes feature close-ups on the violence and only 15% of scenes contain blood and gore. Explicit or graphic violence contributes to desensitization and can enhance fear.

• *There are some notable differences in the presentation of violence across television channels.* Public broadcasting presents violent programs least often (18%) and those violent depictions that appear pose the least risk of harmful effects. Premium cable channels present the highest percentage of violent programs (85%) and those depictions often pose a greater risk of harm than do most violent portrayals. Broadcast networks present violent programs less frequently (44%) than the industry norm (57%), but when they present violence its contextual features are just as problematic as those on most other channels.

• *There are also some important differences in the presentation of violence across types of television programs.* Movies are more likely to present violence in realistic settings (85%), and to include blood and gore in violent scenes (28%) than other program types. The contextual pattern of violence in children's programming also poses concern. Children's programs are the least likely of all genres to show the long-term negative consequences of violence (5%), and they frequently portray violence in a humorous context (67%).

RATINGS AND ADVISORIES

The first year (1994–1995) of studies examined how ratings and advisories are currently being used on television and explored the role that different types of ratings and advisories play in the viewing decisions of children, parents and university undergraduates. Nearly 300 elementary and middle school children (from 5 to 14 years old) participated in the experiments, and an additional 70 parent-child pairs discussed which television programs the child would watch during an experiment.

The content analysis of the sample of televised programming revealed that:

- Very few shows (less than 4%) use advisories, such as "viewer discretion advised," and the content that prompted the concern is rarely indicated.
- The majority of movies broadcast on the three premium channels (56%) employ content codes to indicate the presence of violence.
- Among programs that contain violence, only 15% are preceded with an advisory or any sort of content code.
- Most (81%) of the movies on premium cable channels have Motion Picture Association of America ratings.

The experiments suggest that ratings and advisories can influence children's program choices:

- For boys (and particularly older boys, age 10–14), "parental discretion" advisories and "PG-13" and "R" ratings made programs and movies more attractive.
- For girls (and particularly younger girls, age 5–9), "viewer discretion" advisories made programs less attractive.

Beyond the impact of age and sex, several characteristics of the children were found to be related to their choices of programs:

- Children whose parents generally exerted guidance over their TV viewing were less likely to choose programs labeled as problematic, i.e., with advisories or PG-13 and R ratings.
- Children who had been frightened by a television show in the past were less interested in viewing programs with advisories or movies rated "PG-13" or "R".
- Children who reported engaging in more aggression-related behaviors showed more interest in programs with advisories.

ASSESSING TELEVISION'S ANTI-VIOLENCE MESSAGES

Only 4% of violent programs employ a strong anti-violence theme. Further, only 13% of reality programs that depict violence present any alternatives to violence or ways that violence can be avoided.

Seven studies tested responses to a sample of 15 anti-violence public service announcements (PSAs) created by the television industry, and an award-winning program promoting conflict resolution. More than 200 adolescents drawn from a middle school, a training school for boys, and a university viewed and responded to the anti-violence messages. These are the preliminary findings:

- Viewers, on average, rated 9 of the 15 anti-violence PSAs as interesting.
- No evidence was found that either the anti-violence program or PSAs significantly altered the adolescents' attitudes toward the appropriateness of using violence to resolve conflicts.
- Most anti-violence slogans such as "stop the violence" appeared to promote positions already held by viewers, even those with a history of violent behavior.
- Narrative or dramatic form PSAs were more interesting to audiences than "talking heads" but also were more frequently misinterpreted.
- Although some celebrity endorsers stimulated interest, their lack of credibility, especially those who were per-

ceived as promoting violence in real life or in their jobs (e.g., sports, acting), sometimes confused or undermined the anti-violence messages.

- Messages promoting pacifist themes, such as "just walk away" were not realistic to adolescents who had experience with violence, but scored better with younger, middle school students who had less experience with violence.

- Young people may be more affected by depictions of paralysis and family suffering than death as potential consequences of violence.

- Network promotions and sponsor tags attached to the PSAs appeared to compete for valuable time and audience attention.

> "Critics of violence on television . . .
> ought to admit that the situation is
> improving."

THE AMOUNT OF VIOLENCE ON TELEVISION HAS BEEN EXAGGERATED

John Leo

In February 1996, media scholars released the first report of the National Television Violence Study, which criticized the prevalence of violence on television. In the following viewpoint, John Leo takes issue with the study and its statistical conclusions. For instance, Leo maintains, the study found violence in 57 percent of all television programs surveyed, but this figure relies on an overly broad definition of violence. The amount of graphic and gratuitous violence presented on television is actually far less than critics claim, he argues, and has been declining from past levels. Leo is a syndicated columnist and a contributing editor to *U.S. News & World Report*.

As you read, consider the following questions:

1. What distinctions does Leo make between the different types of violence depicted on television?
2. How does Leo respond to the National Television Violence Study's complaint that violence on television often goes unpunished?
3. What potential problems does Leo foresee with the use of V-chip technology?

Reprinted from John Leo, "Good Drama, Not the Krazy Kat Kind," *U.S. News & World Report*, February 26, 1996, by permission. Copyright 1996 U.S. News & World Report.

Critics of violence on television are on the right track, but they ought to admit that the situation is improving. The best of the current [1996] crop of network crime shows, for instance, are nearly violence free. In the '70s and '80s, on-screen shootings and miscellaneous mayhem seemed routine.

But take a look at current shows like "Law and Order," "Homicide" and "NYPD Blue." As a matter of policy, "Law and Order" never shows the crime that launches the program. It just shows the investigation and trial. "Homicide" and "NYPD Blue" are brilliant shows that concentrate on relationships among their main characters. They don't depend on frenetic action and almost never put a violent act on screen. Even the deeply tedious "Murder One," which works hard at creating an atmosphere of sleaze and menace, has had only a few fleeting images of violence in the thousand or so weeks it seems to have been on ABC. Compare these crime shows with, let's say, "Miami Vice" and other high-body-count programs of the recent past.

There are still some shoot'em-ups and kick-boxing festivals, and violent shows from past seasons are still popping up as re-runs, but on new prime-time series, violence is in decline.

This is not the view of the authors of the big new National Television Violence Study, which was released in February 1996 just before the telecommunications bill was signed, mandating the establishment of a rating system and the inclusion of a V-chip censorship device in every new TV set. The study reports that 57 percent of all TV programs contain violence. But this is an example of how polemical studies are being based on questionable statistics. The 57 percent statistic depends on a very broad definition of violence that turns the four good shows mentioned above into serious offenders. In the study, a brief shot of a dead body counts as violence. So does a credible threat of physical force. This means that a threat to punch someone in the nose could count as much as an on-screen decapitation in determining violent content. So would the cliché shot of a woman wheeling a baby carriage across a street as a speeding car comes along in the distance. Even if the car swerves away, the scene could be listed as violent.

MUDDLING THE ISSUE

Surely this muddies the issue. Our children are unlikely to be lured into a life of violence by glimpsing a body on TV or by I'm-going-to-punch-you barroom rhetoric. We want to guard against graphic violence and violence portrayed as emotionally satisfying, important to masculine identity or as an acceptable way of resolving conflicts. Mixing this violence with images of possible danger—cars that might or might not crash—just confuses the issue.

Also, 46 percent of all TV violence listed in the study turns out to be in cartoons. Well, yes, cartoon makers should move away from routinely violent themes, but the sufferings of Wile E. Coyote at the hands of the Roadrunner do not really preach or rationalize real-life violence. One executive said: "Are we really going to give Bugs Bunny an R rating?"

An NBC Executive Defends Network Programming

When one examines the facts rather than becoming distracted by the rhetoric, it becomes clear that network television is not an appropriate primary target for those concerned with violence in society.

First, the amount of programming on network television that could even arguably be said to contain some violent material is only a tiny fraction of the thousands of hours of entertainment programming offered to viewers each year. For example, during [May 1993], . . . the vast majority of NBC's programming consisted of news, sports, sitcoms, soap operas and game shows devoid of violence. Only a minuscule percentage of the roughly 400 hours of programming offered by NBC—all movies or serious dramas exhibited after 9:00 p.m.—contained some action material that could conceivably be labelled "violent," and, we submit, it was not gratuitous. More to the point, during the May sweeps all ten most watched programs on NBC among children (2–11) were non-violent situation comedies. . . .

Second, the limited depictions of violence on network TV are generally not inappropriate or excessive, but are essential to the development of drama, appear principally in programs for an adult audience, and generally are shown later in the evening.

Third, the primary concern is with the viewing of violent material by children and children simply do not watch network programs designed for adults. Of the top 30 network programs among children, none could reasonably be construed as violent. On the other hand, NBC's highest rated police drama, "Law & Order," ranks 141st among children.

Warren Littlefield, *Violence on Television: Hearings Before the U.S. House of Representatives Subcommittee on Telecommunications and Finance,* 1993.

Other statistics drain away more credibility. The report says violence goes unpunished in almost three out of four scenes. But to avoid being in this category, the violence must be shown to be punished in the same scene in which it occurs. This would turn every TV drama into a version of the old Krazy Kat cartoons—as soon as the mouse conks the cat with a brick, somebody else immediately pounds the mouse over the head with a heavy mallet.

The study is right, however, in concentrating on the fictional aftermath of TV's violence. Few of us really want a moment of heavy moralizing after each aggressive act, but it's reasonable to expect that the violence will be treated in a way that reflects the disastrous and lingering effects it has in real life. Some insist that TV mirrors reality. But as former CBS chief Howard Stringer said, "Let us reflect that reality more skillfully and honestly," with the pain accounted for, too.

LIMITS OF THE V-CHIP

The V-chip may or may not turn out to be as effective as its advocates say. But it is essentially diversionary. The chip is a legally dubious, complicated, distant and privatized solution that puts parents in the uncomfortable position of using technology against their children. One sensible cautionary note in the recent violence study is that warnings about violent programs discourage girls from trying to watch but encourage boys to do so. The chip will inevitably make many children more eager to see violent shows, and they'll do so on older TV sets, on videotape or by learning to disable the V-chip.

Technology is no substitute for lobbying on behalf of good TV programming. Where violence is necessary to tell a story, it can be pushed to later hours. Where it is gratuitous, it ought to disappear. This has already started to happen, partly because the industry is working to attract women to shows that traditionally have had a lot of violence. Since women are far less interested than men are in car crashes and explosions, the female factor has pushed crime shows away from easy violence and toward character development. And the shows are much better for it.

Let the V-chips fall where they may. If we want honest, mature television, public opinion is always better than a technological fix.

|"Violence on television and in the
movies is damaging to children."

MEDIA VIOLENCE HARMS CHILDREN

Madeline Levine

Madeline Levine is a psychologist and the author of *Viewing Violence: How Media Violence Affects Your Child's and Adolescent's Development*, from which the following viewpoint is taken. Levine argues that the violence depicted on television and in motion pictures has been proven to be damaging to children's social and psychological development. She asserts that media violence contributes to the youth crime rate by providing encouragement and instruction in antisocial and violent behavior. Media company executives, she concludes, are failing to meet their social responsibility to provide America's youth with a healthy culture.

As you read, consider the following questions:
1. What has forty years of research established about media violence, according to Levine?
2. According to Levine, how much television do American children watch?
3. What is the agenda of commercial television, in the author's opinion?

The debate is over.

Violence on television and in the movies is damaging to children. Forty years of research conclude that repeated exposure to high levels of media violence teaches some children and adolescents to settle interpersonal differences with violence, while teaching many more to be indifferent to this solution. Under the media's tutelage, children at younger and younger ages are using violence as a first, not a last, resort to conflict.

RESEARCH FINDINGS

Locked away in professional journals are thousands of articles documenting the negative effects of media, particularly media violence, on our nation's youth. Children who are heavy viewers of television are more aggressive, more pessimistic, weigh more, are less imaginative, less empathic, and less capable students than their lighter-viewing counterparts. With an increasing sense of urgency, parents are confronting the fact that the "real story" about media violence and its effects on children has been withheld.

Speaking in 1992 before the U.S. Senate Committee on Governmental Affairs, Leonard Eron, one of the country's foremost authorities on media and children, said:

> There can no longer be any doubt that heavy exposure to televised violence is one of the causes of aggressive behavior, crime and violence in society. The evidence comes from both the laboratory and real-life studies. Television violence affects youngsters of all ages, of both genders, at all socio-economic levels and all levels of intelligence. The effect is not limited to children who are already disposed to being aggressive and is not restricted to this country.

Every major group concerned with children has studied and issued position papers on the effects of media violence on children. The Surgeon General's Scientific Advisory Committee on Television and Social Behavior, the National Institute of Mental Health, the U.S. Attorney General's Task Force on Family Violence, the American Psychological Association, the American Academy of Pediatrics, and the National Parent Teachers Association have all called for curbing television and movie violence. Their findings represent the inescapable conclusions of decades of social science research. Doctors, therapists, teachers, and youth workers all find themselves struggling to help youngsters who, influenced by repeated images of quick, celebratory violence, find it increasingly difficult to negotiate the inevitable frustrations of daily life.

America has become the most violent nation in the industrialized world. Homicide is the leading cause of death for large segments of our country's youth, and we have more young men in prison than any other country in the world. The roots of violence in our society are complex. We are well informed about the contributions of poverty, child abuse, alcoholism, and drug abuse, but we must also consider the role played by the images that our children see on the screen during their three and a half hours of daily viewing.

A major gap exists between research findings and what the public knows about the harmful effects of media violence on children. This is not surprising. Public education often lags behind research, especially when economic stakes are high. Tobacco executives, for instance, are still insisting that "the scientific proof isn't in yet to link smoking and cancer." The entertainment industry stands to lose a great deal of money if violence, a particularly cheap and reliable form of entertainment, becomes less popular.

THE MEDIA INDUSTRY

Ordinarily when science discovers a matter of pressing public concern, it relies on the cooperation of the media to ensure that this information reaches a wide audience. Much of the success of the antismoking campaign was due to the media's active efforts at educating the public. Similarly, the media have played a significant role in educating Americans about the advantages of wearing seat belts, the need for child car seats, and the inadvisability of drinking and driving. As a result, we have seen a significant reduction in children and teenagers dying in motor vehicle accidents. Yet violence among youngsters and teenagers has skyrocketed. Researchers speak with one voice in telling us that this is partly due to the incessant glamorization of violence in the media. However, the entertainment industry's self-protective stance has resulted in these findings being ignored, denied, attacked, or misrepresented.

In May 1995, presidential hopeful Bob Dole delivered a blistering attack on the entertainment industry. "A line has been crossed—not just of taste but of human dignity and decency," admonished the senator. He called for an end to the "mainstreaming of deviancy." While freely admitting that he had not personally seen much of what he attacked, and while seeming to ignore the paradox between calling for an end to violent images while simultaneously supporting a repeal of the ban on assault weapons, Dole struck a chord of national discontent. Headlines across the country announced, "Dole Scolds Entertainment Industry."

In typical punch and parry fashion, the entertainment industry responded within hours. "Hollywood Scoffs at Dole's Rebuke of Show Business," proclaimed feature articles the next day. Using characteristic hyperbole, director Oliver Stone called Senator Dole "a modern-day McCarthy." But of the dozens of articles crossing my desk in this frenzy of accusations and counteraccusations, not one dealt with substantive issues. The entertainment industry can ill afford to "scoff" at the legitimate concerns of parents who feel that their children are awash in images of violence and cruelty. Nor can concerned citizens simply "rebuke" the entertainment industry without being knowledgeable about the problems. Informed dialogue precedes change. The importance of the effects of media violence on child development is far too great to be abandoned to the arena of parental grumbling and political opportunity.

MEDIA VIOLENCE AND CRIME

It seems that we are regularly presented with evidence connecting horrible crimes with exposure to the media:

> Serial killer Nathaniel White described how he killed his first female victim while imitating a scene from the movie *Robocop II*: "I seen him cut somebody's throat then take the knife and slit down the chest to the stomach and leave the body in a certain position. With the first person I killed I did exactly what I saw in the movie." ["Do Movies, Music Trigger Violent Acts?" *Newsday*, August 10, 1992.]

> In New York City, a grammar school child sprayed a Bronx office building with gunfire and explained to an astonished police sergeant that he learned how to load his Uzi-like gun because "I watch a lot of television." [M. Chen, *The Smart Parent's Guide to KIDS' TV*, 1994.]

> Nine-year-old Olivia Niemi was sexually assaulted with a discarded beer bottle on a deserted beach in San Francisco. The four girls who took part in the attack said they were imitating a scene from *Born Innocent*, an NBC television movie they watched three days before committing the crime. The movie, which takes place in a girl's reform school, shows a new inmate cornered by four girls and graphically raped with the handle of a plumber's helper. ["Do Movies, Music Trigger Violent Acts?" *Newsday*, August 10, 1992.]

It is time to move past the debate of whether or not the entertainment industry is "responsible" for these crimes. The question is not whether the media are the cause of crimes like these (they aren't), but whether the media are an important ingredient in the multiple causation of crime (they are). Violence is most frequently the endpoint of a confluence of personal, social, and environmental factors. Television has become a powerful environmental source of behaviors, attitudes, and values. In many homes it threatens the traditional triumvirate of socialization—family, school, and church. *Excessive and gratuitous media violence is an easily reversible contributor to crime.* Quite simply, we need to tell our children stories that will contribute to their healthy development and enhance positive behaviors, rather than allowing the media to encourage negative ones.

THE INFLUENCE OF TELEVISION

By the time they graduate high school, children will have spent 50 percent more time in front of a television set than in front of a teacher. The average American household has television turned on more than seven hours a day, and the average American child watches three to four hours a day. The vast majority of this time is spent watching programs not targeted to a children's audience—game shows, soap operas, and MTV. Television makes no distinctions among viewers. If you are four years old and able to turn on the television, then you are privy to the same information as a fourteen-year-old or a forty-year-old. Television has changed the nature of childhood; it has eradicated many of the traditional barriers that protected children from the harsh facts of adult life. No wonder youngsters who are heavy viewers of television are more pessimistic than light viewers! They have been exposed to a world of violence, sex, commercialism, and betrayal far beyond their emotional capacities. . . .

George Gerbner, dean emeritus of the Annenberg School of Communication, believes that television "tells most of the stories to most of the people, most of the time." Television "cultivates" the viewer's perceptions of society, encouraging the belief that the real world is more or less like the fictionalized world of television. Television has become the melting pot of the twentieth century. It provides us with a shared set of beliefs and assumptions about how the world works. Television is such a fundamental part of life that one in four Americans say they wouldn't surrender their sets for a million dollars.

Network executives are quick to exploit our sense that television is a kind of cultural glue binding us together as a nation. In a *TV Guide* interview, Judy Price, vice president for children's programming at CBS, said, "A kid can't be the only one on the playground not to watch *Power Rangers.*" This statement highlights one of the prime objectives of media promotion. In addition to making things familiar and desirable, the media must create an appearance of social necessity. "A kid can't be the only one on the playground not to watch *Power Rangers*" implies that the child who is prevented from partaking in this quintessential American experience will be denied full participation in the social life of his or her peer group. While shared media experiences are certainly part of group conversation at playgrounds, workplaces, and homes around the country, parents should not be made to feel guilty when they act to protect their children from excessively violent programming. . . .

THE AGENDA OF COMMERCIAL TELEVISION

Television itself should not be demonized. It can serve as an effective instrument for human development and enrichment. Wonderful programs, including many on the Public Broadcasting Service (PBS), have proven that television can teach children new skills, enlarge their worldview, and promote prosocial attitudes and behaviors. But commercial television has a different agenda from personal and cultural development. Its agenda is to round up the largest and most affluent audience it can and deliver that audience to an advertiser.

Advertisers like programs with good track records and proven formulas for gaining an audience. That is why so much of what television offers appears repetitive and predictable. We may have access to hundreds of stations, but in fact the kinds of stories we see are surprisingly limited. As a result, television cultivates a common perspective. All too frequently that perspective includes a reliance on violence as a habitual, acceptable, and even admirable way of resolving conflict. This trivializes the enormous human toll that violence always exacts.

The media, as major disseminators of attitudes, assumptions, and values, can ill afford to ignore their responsibilities while asserting their rights. While the National Rifle Association insists that "guns don't kill people; people kill people," the fact is that people do it with guns. Similarly, television doesn't kill people, but it provides the ideas, the social sanction, and often even the instruction that encourages antisocial behavior. Those who profit from the enormous opportunities for financial gain and status that the entertainment industry provides must act as citizens as well as business people. And it is the responsibility of all citizens, not just parents, to provide America's children with a culturally healthy environment.

The Power of the Media

The effects of the media are not trivial. For example, it is well known that suicide rates increase after the suicide of a celebrity if there is extensive media coverage. The highly publicized suicide of Kurt Cobain, lead singer for the rock group Nirvana, resulted in many copycat suicides of mostly male adolescents. "When Kurt Cobain died, I died with him" was the note left by an eighteen-year-old who, along with two other friends, executed a suicide pact following Cobain's death. This is not to suggest that the news should not have been reported. But science has provided us with enough research to be able to predict that the kind of sensational and repeated coverage that Cobain's suicide received was bound to result in an increase in adolescent suicides. Parents need to be aware that sensational coverage of crime and suicide by young celebrities can be emotionally devastating for vulnerable teens. Parental awareness, supervision, and discussion are critical variables in heading off additional tragedies.

While examples of copycat crimes are particularly distressing, they underscore the power of the media that reach into virtually every household in America. Setting social norms can never be considered a "trivial" task. If you are elderly, it is not trivial that the media insist on reducing you to a dotty simpleton. If you are an African American, it is not trivial that the media vacillate between worshiping you as a sports hero, laughing at you as a buffoon, and reviling you as a thug. If you are a woman, it is not trivial that every female newscaster must be ten or twenty years younger than her male counterpart. If you are a parent who tries to convey the values of hard work and good education to your children, it is not trivial that Beavis and Butt-head have become the supermodels of teenage sloth and indifference.

Images have consequences, often distressing and even tragic ones. My eleven-year-old son and I turned on the news one evening to hear a quick disclaimer about "disturbing images" followed by scenes of dead and critically injured children. In a neighboring community, a van had slammed into a school playground killing one child and critically injuring several others. In the two seconds it took for me to reach over and change channels, those blood-soaked images were burned into our minds. That night my son had great difficulty sleeping and many nightmares. Were those scenes necessary? As news, did that footage teach us anything we need to know about the world or how to conduct our lives? I don't believe it did. Rather, I believe the television station was following the time-honored bromide "If it bleeds, it leads." Media executives who invoke First Amendment rights to justify such irresponsible programming are cowards. Grant Tinker, before becoming president of NBC, called poor television programming "a national crime" and suggested that network executives who did not live up to their responsibilities be jailed.

RIGHTS AND RESPONSIBILITIES

The basis of all societies is a reasonably shared set of values. We may define ourselves individually as Democrats or Republicans, liberals or conservatives, antigovernment or progovernment. Surveys show, however, that most Americans agree that there is a basic set of values that define our society. These include loyalty, responsibility, family, integrity, and courage. It is respect for individual rights, accompanied by a tolerance for diversity, that has characterized America since its founding.

The word *rights* came up repeatedly in my discussions with various media executives: individual rights, creative rights, and, most predictably, First Amendment rights. I am not a political scientist and this incessant referral to First Amendment rights as a way of deflecting criticism sent me scurrying to my son's high school social studies text to refamiliarize myself with the Constitution and the Bill of Rights. I had almost forgotten that there is a Preamble to the Constitution which puts forth the overarching principles of our democracy. In the Preamble there is no mention of rights. Rather, the tone and language recognize that America was founded on the notion of communal responsibility rather than individual rights. The Preamble talks of "*common* defense" and "*general* welfare."

The Bill of Rights, the first ten amendments to the Constitution, is familiar to the public. Whether it's the gun lobby invoking a self-serving version of the Second Amendment (which never said that some desperate, unemployed eighteen-year-old is entitled to an arsenal of semiautomatic weaponry, but rather that a "well-regulated militia" is entitled to bear arms) or First Amendment absolutists like director Oliver Stone, who echoes the sentiments of many in the entertainment industry when he equates criticism with censorship, America has turned her attention from responsibilities to rights. Rights are not entitlements, they are immunities. None of us, whether we are parents, politicians, media executives, or special-interest groups, can afford to forget that along with the extraordinary range of rights that we enjoy in this country is an equally extraordinary range of responsibilities.

When executives in the entertainment industry insist that profits come before responsibility, they do not live up to their commitment to serve the public. When we as parents allow our children to sit and watch hours of thoughtless violence, we do not live up to our commitment to protect and nurture our children. America's children are being hurt. They are hurt when they are the victims or perpetrators of mindless violence, illustrated and glorified by the media. They are hurt when they see the world as a corrupt and frightening place in which only consumer goods bring satisfaction and peace of mind. They are hurt when they have become so dependent on rapid-fire, prefabricated visual effects that they can no longer conjure up their own images or dream their own dreams. It is time to stop hurting our most vulnerable population. It is time to start protecting our children.

"If it weren't so pervasive an idea, the suggestion that those who watch MTV and talk shows or buy rap CDs are primed to commit mayhem would seem idiotic."

MEDIA VIOLENCE DOES NOT HARM CHILDREN

Jon Katz

Jon Katz is a media critic, a novelist, and a contributing editor of *Wired*. In the following viewpoint, taken from his book *Virtuous Reality*, Katz argues that media violence is not responsible for social problems such as youth crime. He contends that "mediaphobes"—including frightened parents, opportunistic politicians, and journalists—have unfairly accused the media of corrupting young people. The true causes of youth crime and violence, Katz maintains, include lax gun-control laws, poverty, and single-parent households.

As you read, consider the following questions:

1. What percentage of Americans believe that television is most responsible for youth violence, according to a *New York Times* survey cited by Katz?
2. Why have journalists been reluctant to probe the true causes of urban violence, according to Katz?
3. What has Harvard psychiatrist Robert Coles determined about the influence of media violence, according to the author?

A central tenet of the Mediaphobe is that guns don't kill people; unwholesome movies, tabloid telecasts, video games and rap music do. That new media are not only corrosive and decivilizing but literally dangerous. . . .

Opportunistic politicians and eager journalists convince millions that culture, not social trauma, causes violence.

FILMS AND VIOLENCE

The 1995 firebombing of a New York City subway station was a classic example. Several would-be thieves squirted flammable liquid into a Queens token booth, causing it to explode. The clerk inside later died from his burns. The attack followed by two weeks the release of the movie *Money Train*, including a scene in which a pyromaniac squirts flammable liquid into token booths (though the celluloid clerks escape injury). *The New York Times* said the movie joined a "long list of films and television shows blamed for prompting acts of violence." It included the Martin Scorsese film *Taxi Driver*, cited by prosecutors as the inspiration for the attempted assassination of President Reagan by John W. Hinckley, Jr., in 1981; Oliver Stone's *Natural Born Killers*, said by the Utah police to have prompted a teenager to kill his stepmother and half sister; and *The Program*, blamed for the deaths of two teenagers because this 1993 movie showed drunken football players lying down in traffic.

Critics, reporters and politicians jumped on the *Money Train* parallels, with [Kansas senator and 1996 Republican presidential candidate] Bob Dole one of the first out of the gate. "The American people have a right to voice their outrage," he told reporters. "For those in the entertainment industry who too often engage in a pornography of violence as a way to sell movie tickets, it is time for some serious soul-searching." Dole, an opponent of gun control, did not comment on the M-1 carbine, with a clip holding seventeen cartridges, that was found at the scene of the fire-bombing. Nor did he have much to say when a couple of weeks later, the district attorney and the police said the attack had not been inspired by the film at all.

This distraction is not just a matter of journalistic harrumphing. It is a significant distortion of a major American social problem, with enormous impact on the way our society does— or doesn't—react to violence. "Americans have a starkly negative view of popular culture," *The New York Times* found in a survey taken in August 1995, "and blame television more than any other single factor for teenage sex and violence."

Twenty-one percent said television was most responsible for

teenage violence, compared with only 13 percent who blamed lack of supervision, 8 percent who blamed the breakdown of family, and 7 percent who blamed drugs. In all, a third put the primary blame on some aspect of popular culture.

WHO'S GETTING HURT BY WHAT

As it happened, weeks before the subway attack, the Justice Department released a crucial report on juvenile crime. Nearly one in four people arrested for weapons crimes in America were juveniles (23 percent), the report said, compared with 16 percent in 1974. Such juvenile arrests more than doubled, from fewer than 30,000 to more than 61,000 between 1985 and 1993, while adult arrests for the same crimes grew by only one-third. Weapons offenses include the illegal use, possession, trafficking, carrying, manufacturing, importing and exporting of guns, ammunition, silencers, explosives and some types of knives. The statistics closely mirrored the surge in violent youth crimes, reported the federal officials. Teenage violence, particularly with guns, has been rising steadily since 1985, even as the number of teenagers nationwide has been declining.

But the Justice Department report got little attention in the media, compared with the furor over *Money Train*. It was . . . another purported link—advanced by politicians and the eager news media—between culture and danger. Even a meticulous newspaper reader or television watcher would naturally conclude that movies have more to do with violence than guns, poverty or drugs—and that without such graphic portrayals, the kids with the M-1 wouldn't have torched a token booth.

The fact is that during the past couple of years, as mediaphobes have decried the supposedly pernicious effects of pop culture, violent crime has decreased, not grown, in most of America. Homicides showed the largest drop in thirty-five years—12 percent—during the first six months of 1995, continuing the decline seen in 1994. In both big cities and suburbs, there were double-digit decreases in the murder rate. New York City, which has logged five successive years of declining crime, has returned to levels of homicide not seen since 1971.

If it weren't so pervasive an idea, the suggestion that those who watch MTV and talk shows or buy rap CDs are primed to commit mayhem would seem idiotic. Clearly, crime rises and falls for other reasons.

Yet violence among the young—who are presumed by mediaphobes to be particularly vulnerable to forces like lyrics and action movies—has been, sadly, on the rise. The urban underclass in particular—mostly black and Latino—has been engulfed in a wave of escalating violence. A slight dip (of less than 3 percent) in the juvenile violent crime rate in 1995, the first in a decade, shouldn't obscure that fact.

CRIME AND ITS CAUSES

According to the National Criminal Justice Reference Service, homicide is now the second leading cause of death among young Americans. But it's hardly uniformly distributed. From 1986 to 1989, for example, the homicide rate for white twenty-to-twenty-four-year-olds was 12 deaths per 100,000. Among blacks, it was 72 per 100,000. Though black males age twelve to twenty-four represent 1.3 percent of the population, the FBI's Uniform Crime Reports for 1992 show that they experienced 17.2 percent of single-victim homicides. That translates into a homicide rate of 114.9 killings per 100,000 black males of that age, more than ten times the rate for their white male counterparts.

Scholars like Andrew Hacker, Christopher Jencks, Elijah Anderson and Cornel West have meticulously documented the origins of this tragedy—racism, disintegrating family structures, the rise of births among single teenage mothers, lack of job training and economic opportunity, deteriorating schools, the proliferation of weapons, the drug epidemic. Among the white suburban middle class, by contrast, violence remains relatively rare. And it is the affluent middle class, of course, that is targeted by marketers of CDs (including rap), cable and computer technology. Underclass kids can't afford computers or piles of CDs.

We know what's killing young people, and it isn't lyrics, cartoons or computers. . . .

Covering the true causes of urban violence would mean taking on some of the most difficult and sensitive issues in American life—race, poverty, welfare systems, law enforcement. Many journalists, like academics, have come to fear such issues; probing them inevitably brings accusations of racism or some other form of bigotry. Blaming violence on media and culture is easier and safer, both for journalists and for opportunistic politicians. . . .

MOTION PICTURES AND CHILDREN

One of the reasons we have so much trouble understanding complicated issues like purported connections between culture and violence . . . is that so many "experts" are thrown at us, often peddling contradictory conclusions.

But some experts have better credentials than others.

Harvard psychiatrist Robert Coles, no fan of TV violence, has been studying and writing about the moral, spiritual and developmental lives of children for much of his life. His works have been widely praised and circulated as ground-breaking, insightful looks at kids' complex inner lives. Parents worried about the impact culture has on their kids should ignore the headlines and read The Moral Life of Children. They would know more and feel better.

A young moviegoer, Coles writes, can repeatedly be exposed to the "excesses of a Hollywood genre"—sentimentality, violence, the misrepresentation of history, racial stereotypes, pure simple-mindedness—and emerge unscathed intellectually as well as morally. In fact, sometimes these images help the child to "sort matters out, stop and think about what is true and what is not by any means true—in the past, in the present." The child, says Coles, "doesn't forget what he's learned in school, learned at home, from hearing people talk in his family and his neighborhood."

Culture offers important moments for moral reflection, and it ought not to be used as an occasion for "overwrought psychiatric comment," Coles warns, or for making banal connections between films and "the collective American conscience."

But it is. All the time.

MEDIA VIOLENCE AND MINORITIES

This discussion—of culture, morality and violence—is made more difficult because of not irrational fears on the part of minorities that their children will be demonized and stereotyped as lawless and dangerous, when only a small percentage are involved in crime or violence. Understandably, black leaders want to project more positive images of African-American life than the young black men so often seen in handcuffs on the local news.

But black political leaders who insist that violence is a universal American problem equally affecting blacks and whites, or who point to media and popular culture as its primary causes, are hardly advancing any racial goals or staving off prejudice. They simply make it easier for the majority of Americans to ignore poverty, bad schools and guns—since those problems are purportedly less to blame than *Money Train*. Unwittingly, this particular brand of mediaphobe conspires to keep Americans ignorant about what really causes violence and what can be done to prevent it.

"Scientifically sound studies from diverse perspectives . . . link media violence to violent attitudes, values, and behaviors."

STUDIES HAVE ESTABLISHED THAT MEDIA VIOLENCE CAUSES VIOLENCE

John P. Murray

The question of whether or not violence on television leads to violent attitudes and behavior in real life has been the topic of numerous sociological and psychological studies. In the following viewpoint, John P. Murray argues that such studies have conclusively demonstrated that violence in the media, especially television, is a contributing cause of violence in American society. Murray is a professor and director of the School of Family Studies and Human Services at Kansas State University. He has written numerous articles and books about television, including *Big World, Small Screen: The Role of Television in American Society*.

As you read, consider the following questions:
1. What are the differences and similarities between film violence and television violence, according to Murray?
2. What examples does the author give of instances when people have imitated acts of violence depicted in movies or television?
3. According to Murray, in what three main ways does television violence affect children and adults?

The impact of media violence on youth has been a topic of intense discussion and debate in the United States for the better part of this century. Beginning in the 1920s and '30s, there were questions raised about the influence of crime and violence portrayed in comic books, movies, radio serials, and, by the 1950s, television. For example, the initial studies and concerns about movies were outlined as early as W.W. Charters's (1933) monograph *Motion Pictures and Youth: A Summary*. In each instance, the concerns about violence are similar: Does media violence influence the attitudes and behavior of the youngest members of our society? Of course, similar questions could be asked about the influence of media violence on adults, but most of the social concern and much of the scientific research has been focused on children and youth.

A Perennial Issue

Despite almost 70 years of research on media violence, it is still possible to spark a lively discussion of this issue. Moreover, each new form of media—such as video games or the Internet—inspires renewed discussion of the issue of media violence. If the hypothetical "Martian" were to scan the 20th-century discussions of media violence, he/she/it would be appalled by the circularity and indecisiveness of professionals and public policy pundits.

And yet, part of the compelling nature of the media violence discussions is the seemingly transparent relationship between what we see and hear and the way we think and act. Some have argued that this transparent relationship is truly gossamer, whereas others contend that the relationship of media violence and societal violence is substantial and profoundly disturbing. The reason that these two viewpoints can coexist—and have done so for many decades—is the fact that media violence and societal violence are not related in any direct and simple manner, and there are multiple causes for both phenomena.

This viewpoint will explore the relationships between media violence and violence in youth with a focused examination of the issue of television violence. Although there are differences in the intensity, interest, and interpretation of violence found across various media, there are great similarities in the process of effects. On the one hand, the intensity of violence in films is often greater (in terms of the graphic nature and frequency of violent acts) than that found in prime-time television programs. On the other hand, the frequency of contact with film violence is usually less than the frequency of contact with television violence. This is one example of a "trade-off" of frequency of viewing versus intensity of portrayal. So too, adolescents are more likely to encounter graphic film violence than would be the case for very young children. However, young children, who are still in the early stages of learning social roles and standards of acceptable behavior, may be more affected by the frequent depictions of violence on television than the adolescent who is watching a "slasher" film. Of course, the complicating feature in this analysis is the fact that the adolescent sitting in the movie theater was once a child sitting in front of a television set and, therefore, has a long history of exposure to media violence.

IMITATING FILM VIOLENCE

In New York, in the fall of 1995, youths set fire to a subway token booth by spraying a flammable substance through the opening for the change and token slot. The booth exploded and burned the subway attendant. The attendant died in December 1995 as a result of extensive burns. This was one of the more dramatic episodes in a series of attacks that seemed to be related to a recently released movie, *Money Train*, in which a similar act occurred.

A few years earlier in Los Angeles, a filmmaker interviewed a young man who was being held in the Los Angeles County Juvenile Detention Center on a charge of attempted murder. The 16-year-old was asked how it happened, and he replied, "The guy came after me and I had a gun. So, I shot him. I shot him twice. It's easy to get a gun in the 'hood." When asked about his favorite television programs, he said, "I like to watch that show, the *Cops*, or *America's Most Wanted*; I might see some of my friends out there, messin up."

In the late 1970s, when the movie *The Deerhunter* was released, it contained a very graphic portrayal of Russian roulette. While the film was playing in theaters and in video release, there were numerous reports of adolescents, usually males, imitating the Russian roulette scene, often with tragic results. Of course, there were many additional factors that influenced this result, such as watching the video with a group of young males who were drunk, or a history of depression or suicide attempts. Nevertheless, some incidents of death from this film were simply accidents of imitation gone awry.

In the early 1970s, a made-for-television movie called *The Doomsday Flight* contained an easily imitated bomb threat/hostage plot. When the movie was broadcast in the United States, there were numerous bomb threats directed to various airlines. When the movie was sold to an Australian commercial television network, the result was a ransom of one million dollars paid by

Qantas Airlines to save a jetliner en route from Sydney to Hong Kong. (The plot involved a bomb that was activated on takeoff and would detonate when the plane dropped to an altitude of 4,000 feet. In the United States, the bomb threats to the airlines were handled by diverting aircraft to Denver or Mexico City—high-altitude airports. However, Qantas lacked a high-altitude airport for diversion between Sydney and Hong Kong.)

THE EFFECTS OF TELEVISION VIOLENCE

Over 35 years of laboratory and real-life studies provide evidence that televised violence is a cause of aggression among children, both contemporaneously, and over time.

Television violence affects youngsters of all ages, both genders, at all socio-economic levels, and all levels of intelligence.

The effect is not limited to children who are already disposed to being aggressive, and it is not restricted to the United States.

The fact that the same finding of a relation between television violence and aggression in children has been found in study after study, in one country after another, cannot be ignored. The causal effect of television violence on aggression, even though it is not very large, exists.

In my own research, I have found that children who tend to watch aggressive, violent acts on television are more likely to be violent and aggressive as children.

Moreover, those who watched more violent television at age eight are more likely to be more aggressive as adults, with effects lasting well into the middle years.

Among the findings, it was found that subjects who most frequently watched violent television at age eight were more prone to be convicted for more serious crimes by age thirty, to be more aggressive while under the influence of alcohol, and to be more abusive toward their spouses, and harsher in the punishment they administered to their own children.

Leonard Eron, *Violence on Television: Hearings of the U.S. Senate Committee on Commerce, Science, and Transportation*, 1995.

Are these reports of tragic events merely the isolated outcomes of unfortunate circumstances, or are these events simply the more dramatic examples of a subtle and pervasive influence of media violence? . . .

POTENTIAL EFFECTS OF TELEVISION VIOLENCE

What can be said about violence in society and the relationship to media violence? Is there a rational pattern of relationships; a reasonable level of concern about media violence; a systematic body of evidence from research conducted in various settings? The answer is "yes" to all of these questions. Although there are many causes of violence in society, there are scientifically sound studies from diverse perspectives that link media violence to violent attitudes, values, and behaviors.

One of the suggestions about the way in which media violence affects audiences of all ages is that such depictions transmit a sense of acceptance or normativeness about violence in our lives—a confirmation that violence is an acceptable and usual way to resolve conflicts. This is the sense that Leonard Berkowitz uses when he describes the effects of "thoughts" on the manifestation of antisocial behavior, and it is the sense that is captured in his popular article on gun control entitled "When the Trigger Pulls the Finger."

It is important to note that psychologists and psychiatrists involved in media studies do not suggest that violent media are the only cause of violence in society. Rather there are many wellsprings of violent behavior, such as growing up in an abusive home or a violent neighborhood. However, media are one component of a potentially toxic environment for youth, and it is important to understand the roles that media play in youth violence and ways to mitigate these harmful influences. So, what do we know, and what can we do about media violence? In particular, since it is the most pervasive form of media violence in the lives of children and youth, what can be done about television violence?

STUDIES OF MEDIA VIOLENCE

Concern about television violence made its official debut in 1952 with a congressional hearing in the House of Representatives before the Commerce Committee. The following year, in 1953, the first major Senate hearing was held before the Senate Subcommittee on Juvenile Delinquency, headed by Senator Estes Kefauver.

One of the first major reports on media violence was the National Commission on the Causes and Prevention of Violence. The next landmark event occurred when the Surgeon General of the United States released a report in 1972 that concluded that violence on television does influence children who view that programming and does increase the likelihood that viewers will become more aggressive. Not all children are affected, not all children are affected in the same way, but there is evidence that television violence can be harmful to young viewers. Ten years later, the National Institute of Mental Health concluded that violence on television does affect the aggressive behavior of children and there are many more reasons for concern about violence on television. "The research question has moved from asking whether or not there is an effect to seeking explanations for that effect."

In 1992, the American Psychological Association Task Force on Television and Society concluded that 30 years of research confirms the harmful effects of television violence. And, these conclusions were reaffirmed by the American Psychological Association Commission on Violence and Youth.

THREE HARMFUL EFFECTS

How are we affected by television violence? There seem to be three major avenues: direct effects, desensitization, and the Mean World Syndrome:

1. The *direct effects* process suggests that children and adults who watch a lot of violence on television may become more aggressive and/or they may develop favorable attitudes and values about the use of aggression to resolve conflicts.

2. The second effect, *desensitization*, suggests that children who watch a lot of violence on television may become less sensitive to violence in the real world around them, less sensitive to the pain and suffering of others, and more willing to tolerate ever-increasing levels of violence in our society.

3. The third effect, the *Mean World Syndrome*, suggests that children or adults who watch a lot of violence on television may begin to believe that the world is as mean and dangerous in real life as it appears on television, and hence, they begin to view the world as a much more mean and dangerous place. . . .

The broad dimensions of research on television violence over the past 40 years can be described under three categories of research strategies: correlational studies, experimental studies, and field studies. These three rather different approaches to studying the "effects" of violent portrayals in television or film converge on the common conclusion that viewing violence can lead to changes in attitudes, values, and behavior concerning the acceptance and expression of violence.

> "There is no convincing . . . evidence
> that television violence affects
> aggression or crime."

STUDIES HAVE NOT ESTABLISHED A LINK BETWEEN MEDIA VIOLENCE AND VIOLENCE

Jonathan Freedman

Jonathan Freedman is a professor of psychology at the University of Toronto in Ontario, Canada. The following viewpoint is taken from testimony he presented in 1995 before a U.S. Senate committee that was holding hearings on television violence. Freedman argues that, despite the claims made by some media scholars, a direct cause-and-effect relationship between media violence and violence in society has not been demonstrated. In fact, he asserts, the messages taught by television programs may actually discourage viewers from resorting to violence as a way to resolve conflicts.

As you read, consider the following questions:

1. What is the maximum possible effect television violence may have on the violent crime rate, according to Freedman?
2. What messages or lessons are conveyed by most violent television programs, in the author's view?
3. According to Freedman, what two separate social problems do many people confuse?

Reprinted from Jonathan Freedman's testimony in *Television Violence*, a hearing before the U.S. Senate Committee on Commerce, Science, and Transportation, July 12, 1995.

I find myself in a somewhat difficult situation here, since the opening remarks by the members of Congress, and Senators, and Congressmen, and virtually all the remarks by everyone else make it clear that everyone has accepted that watching television violence causes aggression and causes crime.

Before disagreeing with that in a little bit more detail, let me just say that I am here representing no group. I have no connections with the media or television, have never gotten a grant to study this issue. My career in no way depends on it.

I just, in fact, almost accidentally got involved in this question, because I was teaching a course, a graduate course, and wanted a good topic to study, and television violence seemed like a good one, because so many different research methods have been used.

During the course, I read this research, which I had only glanced at before, and five students and five faculty members from various different points of view and disciplines read this research very, very carefully.

A SURPRISING DISCREPANCY

We were first amazed, and then astonished, and then, I must say, dismayed at the discrepancy between what we were reading and what everyone was saying. Because of that, I then decided that I better spend more time reading it. I spent over a year reading every piece of research I could find.

I finally wrote a paper, which was accepted by the leading journal of this kind, by the American Psychological Association. I took the position that the evidence does not support a causal relationship between television violence and aggression.

So the first point I would like to make is that . . . I am convinced that any objective group of scientists who come into this without a preconceived notion, and go through the research very carefully and critically, will conclude that there is no convincing, in fact, no substantial evidence that television violence affects aggression or crime.

I am sure that very few people would want to do that. I do not recommend it. The studies are boring and tedious, and are difficult to read.

But I would be willing to put this to a test, and not have people who have already decided, as heads of committees, but people who have not decided, especially have a jury of experts who do not know anything about the issue to begin with, and let them look at the research.

I think if you do that, you would find that the evidence is, in some sense, laughable.

If a drug company brought in this kind of evidence and said we want to show that this new drug works, and they brought in evidence where you do fourteen comparisons, and two of them are significant, or you have thirty studies, and one or two of them get really strong positive effects, and some of them get the reverse, and most of them get nothing, the Food and Drug Administration (FDA) would certainly not license that drug.

That is the kind of data we are talking about here. I know I cannot convince you of that, but I would be happy to give you examples.

Unfortunately, there are many people who are so committed to this belief that they have intentionally or otherwise over-stated, misrepresented, and distorted the findings. . . .

A SMALL EFFECT

The second point I would like to make is that . . . the effects, even if you accept them, are small. We are not talking about the effect of cigarette smoking on lung cancer, where you get 200, or 300, or 1,000 percent increase of the likelihood of getting cancer.

We are talking maybe 5 percent, maybe 10 percent. It is hard to tell. That is, I do not believe it is anything, but if you accept it at its highest, as they might say in legal circles, it is maybe 5 or 10 percent.

This is not insubstantial, I am not saying it is, but I do not think that these are major effects. It is easier to attack television violence, and I have no great love for it myself, but do not think that you are going to have a big impact.

We do not know the true causes of aggression and crime, but almost everyone who studies this agrees that poverty and racial conflict, discrepancy between what people want and their hopes, the availability of guns, and drug use, and so on, are major causes; probably family breakup, poor child rearing, all of those things are major causes of violence.

We do not really know. But no one seriously suggests that television violence is one of the major causes. It is, at best, a very minor cause.

THE MESSAGES OF TELEVISION

The third point I would like to talk about is why it might not have such a negative effect. . . .

If a commercial has an effect, and makes you buy a particular product, why does watching television violence not have an effect? It is important to understand that children and adults do not imitate blindly, but they learn messages. They accept messages from television.

What is the message they get from most of the violence on television? Typically, it is the bad guys who start the fight. The bad guys are the ones who initiate the violence.

It is very rare that you have a good guy who starts the violence. Good guys will eventually respond, and I will get to that. And also on television, the bad guys lose. They get punished.

THE THERAPEUTIC VALUE OF TELEVISION VIOLENCE

A revealing finding from several studies regarding television viewers and their selections is that, irrespective of program violence levels as determined by objective count, people believe the violence on their favorite action programming is low, while they judge the violence on shows they do not like to be excessive. . . .

People uncritically welcome their own selections of fantasy violence into their minds because they anticipate that content is going to be of some personal benefit. They look forward to feeling better after exposure than they had before, perhaps more tranquil and resolved.

How does such improvement in sentiment happen? It is easy to hypothesize the psychological mechanism: the viewer identifies with the policewoman or the explosives expert or the running back, and aggresses vicariously while the televised figure aggresses under dramatic, sanctioned conditions. Having aggressed if only in the imagination, the viewer feels a modest sense of relief afterwards. Television violence has helped in the harmless discharge of hostile feelings. This is an important service, one that may bring the viewer back to the same type of the content the next time around, if not the same series.

That television violence can relieve aggressive feelings, and do so for large numbers of people, was demonstrated in an extensive (but regrettably overlooked) study by sociologist Steven Messner, published in the February 1986, issue of the respected journal *Social Problems*. His analysis was simplicity itself: looking at the nation's metropolitan areas, Messner compared levels of violence viewing in those markets (determined by Nielsen ratings there for the most violent programs) with subsequent local statistics on violent crime.

The results of his analyses and subanalyses were unanticipated and, he confessed, surprising: "The data consistently indicate that high levels of exposure to violent television content are accompanied by relatively low rates of violent crime." Heightened viewing of violent fantasies was statistically linked to subsiding real-world violence. Could the relationship be any clearer?

Jib Fowles, *Television Quarterly*, vol. 28, no. 1, 1996.

One thing we know is that children learn not to do those things for which they expect to get punished.

The other thing that children learn is that often the good guys respond with violence against violence. Now, this is unfortunate but it probably is a fact of life that it is not easy to deal with someone else's violence without using force yourself.

So that is probably realistic. I admit that that is probably what children learn. They may not learn that is the only way of dealing with it, because there are lots of programs that do it the other way, but that is one thing they learn.

Finally, they learn that those who resort to the violence, the good guys, are almost always those in our society that we expect, in fact, we want to use force to control the bad guys—the police, the FBI, detectives, or self-appointed but recognized characters, such as Batman or the Power Rangers or the Ninja Turtles, all defenders of the good.

They are the ones who use most of the violence. It is rare for the everyday civilian to be the one who is shown resorting to violence. It is much more typical that it is these forces.

So what in the end might the children learn? Do not start violence, you are going to get punished. If violence occurs, you can rely on the good guys to try to do something about it, but you are not the ones that should do it.

Now, I am not saying that is really what happens. I do not know what happens. But I am just trying to make it plausible. Keep in mind that Japan has probably the most violent television on earth, and they have an extremely low rate of violent crime. . . .

Two Different Problems

Many of these speakers . . . seem to be confusing the problem of violence in our society, which I think we can all agree is a serious problem, and the problem of violence on television, which many people do not like—they find it offensive, and would like to get rid of it. But do not equate them. If you got rid of all violence on television tomorrow, and no one ever watched violent television again, you would probably see no change in violent crime.

At the very most, it would be an imperceptible change in the rate of violence and crime in our society. It is just a very, very minor factor.

| "It is in the children's best interest to
listen to lyrics or to watch videos
that are not violent."

VIOLENT MUSIC LYRICS CAN HARM CHILDREN

Frank Palumbo

The following viewpoint is taken from testimony that Frank Palumbo, a pediatrician, presented in 1997 on behalf of the American Academy of Pediatrics (AAP) during congressional hearings on violent content in music lyrics and videos. Palumbo declares that he and other members of the AAP are concerned about how rock and rap songs featuring references to sexual violence, suicide, and other violent themes affect listeners. While he concedes that studies have not definitively proved that listening to violent music leads to violent behavior, he argues that there is significant evidence suggesting that violent lyrics and videos can desensitize young people to real-life violence.

As you read, consider the following questions:

1. How many hours a week do teens listen to music, according to one study cited by Palumbo?
2. What examples of questionable themes and lyrics does the author describe?
3. What recommendations does Palumbo make concerning how society should respond to violent song lyrics and videos?

Reprinted from Frank Palumbo's testimony in *The Social Impact of Music Violence*, a hearing before the U.S. Senate Subcommittee on Oversight of Government Management, Restructuring, and the District of Columbia, November 6, 1997.

Thank you for the opportunity to testify about the social impact of music violence. My name is Dr. Frank Palumbo and I am a practicing pediatrician here in Washington, D.C. I am testifying on behalf of the American Academy of Pediatrics (AAP), an organization of 53,000 primary care pediatricians, pediatric medical subspecialists and pediatric surgical specialists dedicated to the health, safety and well-being of infants, children, adolescents and young adults.

Pediatricians' concern about the impact of music lyrics and music videos on children and youth compelled the AAP Committee on Communications to issue a policy statement on the subject in December 1989, as well as one on media violence in 1995. Policy statements are the official position of the Academy concerning health care issues, and help guide pediatricians in their assessment and treatment of patients.

Pediatricians with a specialty in adolescent medicine are keenly aware of how crucial music is to a teen's identity and how it helps them define important social and subcultural boundaries. One study found that teens listened to music an average of 40 hours per week.

ROCK MUSIC LYRICS

During the past four decades, rock music lyrics have become increasingly explicit—particularly with reference to drugs, sex, violence and, even of greater concern, sexual violence. Heavy metal and rap lyrics have elicited the greatest concern, as they compound the environment in which some adolescents increasingly are confronted with pregnancy, drug use, acquired immunodeficiency syndrome and other sexually transmitted diseases, injuries, homicide and suicide.

For example, Nine Inch Nails released "Big Man with a Gun," with the following lyrics: "I am a big man (yes I am) and I have a big gun; got me a big old dick and I like to have fun: held against your forehead, I'll make you suck it, maybe I'll put a hole in your head; you know, just for the f—k of it . . . I'm every inch a man, and I'll show you somehow; me and my f—king gun; nothing can stop me now; shoot shoot shoot shoot shoot . . ."

Marilyn Manson has quite the way with a lyric: "Who said date rape isn't kind," "The housewife I will beat" and "I slit my teenage wrist" are just a sample from two songs.

THE EFFECTS OF MUSIC

To date, no studies have documented a cause-and-effect relationship between sexually explicit or violent lyrics and adverse behavioral effects; i.e., I'll listen to a song about killing someone and therefore I go out and kill. But we can all acknowledge the overall effect music has on people, including adolescents and children. Otherwise, we wouldn't listen to it. Music wakes us up in the morning, makes us want to dance, soothes us when we're feeling sad and grates on some folks' nerves in the elevator. From infancy to adulthood, it is an integral part of our lives. Mothers sing lullabies to babies, toddlers and children play "ring around the rosie," and teenagers become absorbed in songs they believe help better define them during this rocky transition into adulthood. Make no mistake about it, music can summon a range of emotions, most of which are wonderful. Yet there is some music that communicates potentially harmful health messages, especially when it reaches a vulnerable audience.

If parents in the 50s didn't like Elvis' gyrating hips, those same people would be astounded at how rapidly we've reached the "anything goes" mentality of the 90s. With the advent of [cable television channels] MTV and VH-1, not only do we have to listen to violent lyrics that, for example, degrade women, but we also get to see it acted out in full color. A handful of experimental studies indicate that music videos may have a significant behavioral impact by desensitizing violence and by making teenagers more likely to approve of premarital sex. According to a U.S. Department of Education report, a large percentage of young women and girls have been "subjected to a pattern of overt sexual hostility accompanied by actual or threatened physical contact and the repeated use of obscene or foul language."

An article in the May 1997 issue of the *Archives of Pediatrics and Adolescent Medicine* documented televised music videos with multiple episodes of violence or weapon carrying. Rock's Guns-N-Roses and Beastie Boys each reached 36 violent episodes in performing just one song.

WHAT POLLS REVEAL

A wide majority of adults surveyed in a 1997 report from Public Agenda, "Kids These Days: What Americans Really Think about the Next Generation," decried sex and violence in the media as threatening to the well-being of young people. The report, however, couches this as a problem without a solution. "Given the intense complaints about the media, it is somewhat surprising that only half of those surveyed (49%) think pressuring the entertainment industry to produce movies and music with less violence and sex will be a very effective way to help kids. Perhaps people doubt that the industry will be responsive to public pressure, or wonder just how much influence they as individuals can bring to bear," it states.

CREATING A CULTURE OF VIOLENCE

We don't seem to blink when prominent corporate citizens sell music to our children that celebrates violence, including the murder of police, gang rape, and sexual perversity, including pedophilia. . . .

Consider a song like "Slap-a-Hoe" by the group Dove Shack, distributed by Polygram, which touted the virtues of a machine that automatically smacks a wife or girlfriend into line; or the vile work of the death metal band Cannibal Corpse, distributed through a Sony subsidiary, which recorded one song describing the rape of a woman with a knife and another describing the act of masturbating with a dead woman's head.

These songs and others like them contain some of the most disgusting thoughts I've ever heard, but they are more than just offensive. When combined with all the murder and mayhem depicted by the whole gamut of media, they are helping to create a culture of violence that is increasingly enveloping our children, desensitizing them to consequences and ultimately cheapening the value of human life. . . .

The men and women who run Seagram, Time Warner, Sony, BMG, EMI and Polygram must stop hiding behind the First Amendment and confront the damage some—and I emphasize some—of their products are doing.

We are not talking about censorship, but about citizenship. We're not asking for any government action or bans. We're simply asking whether it is right for Sony, for example, to make money by selling children records by the likes of Cannibal Corpse and rapper MC Eiht, who brags in one obscenity-filled song of using a gun to play connect the dots on his victim's chest. We're asking why a great company like Seagram is continuing to associate itself with Marilyn Manson and the vile, hateful, and nihilistic music he records?

Senator Joseph Lieberman, statement before the Governmental Affairs Committee Subcommittee on Oversight of Government Management, Restructuring, and the District of Columbia, November 6, 1997.

We believe something can and should be done. Poll after poll laments the belief that our country, including its youth, is losing its moral center. Responsibility, respect and discipline are thought to be a thing of the past. Crime and violence have escalated to the point where it is a public health problem. Although there is no one solution, awareness of, and sensitivity to, the potential impact of music lyrics and videos by consumers, the media and the music industry is one important piece of the puzzle. It is in the children's best interest to listen to lyrics or to watch videos that are not violent, sexist, drug-oriented, or antisocial.

The Academy strongly opposes censorship. As a society, however, we have to acknowledge the responsibility parents, the music industry and others have in helping to foster the nation's children.

THE ACADEMY'S RECOMMENDATIONS

Although the evidence is incomplete, based on our knowledge of child and adolescent development, the AAP believes that parents should be aware of pediatricians' concerns about the possible negative impact of music lyrics and videos. The Academy recommends that:

• Research should be developed concerning the impact music lyrics and videos have on the behavior of adolescents and preadolescents.

• The music video industry should be encouraged to produce videos and public service messages with positive themes about relationships, racial harmony, drug avoidance, nonviolence and conflict resolution, sexual abstinence, pregnancy prevention, and avoidance of sexually transmitted diseases.

• Music video producers should be encouraged to exercise sensitivity and self-restraint in what they depict, as should networks in what they choose to air.

• The music industry should develop and apply a system of specific content-labeling of music regarding violence, sex, drugs, or offensive lyrics. For those concerned about the "forbidden fruit" syndrome, only one study has examined the impact of parental advisory labels, and it found that teens were not more likely to be attracted simply because of the labeling. We label the food we eat, and the movies we watch—why not label the music? If labeling is not done voluntarily by the music industry, then regulation should be developed to make it mandatory.

• Performers should be encouraged to serve as positive role models for children and teenagers.

• Pediatricians should join with educators and parents in local and national coalitions to discuss the effects of music lyrics on children and adolescents. The possible negative impact of sexually explicit, drug-oriented, or violent lyrics on compact discs, tapes, music videos and the Internet should be brought to light in the context of any possible behavioral effects.

• Parents should take an active role in monitoring music that their children are exposed to and which they can purchase, as well as the videos they watch. Ultimately, it is the parents' responsibility to monitor what their children listen to and view. Pediatricians should encourage parents to do so.

• Pediatricians should counsel parents to become educated about the media. This means watching television with their children and teenagers, discussing content with them, and initiating the process of selective viewing at an early age. In order to help this process, the Academy has launched Media Matters, a national media education campaign targeted to physicians, parents and youth. The primary goal of the Media Matters campaign is to help parents and children understand and impact upon the sometimes negative effects of images and messages in the media, including music lyrics and videos.

Media Education

Media education includes developing critical thinking and viewing skills, and offering creative alternatives to media consumption. The Academy is particularly concerned about mass media images and messages, and the resulting impact on the health of vulnerable young people, in areas including violence, safety, sexuality, use of alcohol, tobacco, and illicit drugs, nutrition, and self-concept and identity.

For example, if a music video shows violence against women to any degree, a viewer, including young girls, could be led to believe such action is acceptable. If they are educated about the media, the premise in the video would be questioned and hopefully rejected.

Again, let me reiterate the point about a collective solution. Parents, pediatricians, the music industry and others have critical roles in discussing and addressing the increasing amount of violence in society, particularly when it comes to children and adolescents. It is my sincere hope that this hearing will begin a dialogue with all interested parties.

"Many 'good kids' listen to shock rock."

VIOLENT MUSIC LYRICS DO NOT USUALLY CAUSE LASTING HARM

James K. Fitzpatrick

The often-violent content of rock and rap music lyrics and videos troubles many Americans. In the following viewpoint, James K. Fitzpatrick, a public high school teacher and the author of four books, evaluates the impact of violent rock music lyrics on young people. Focusing on the controversial musician Marilyn Manson, Fitzpatrick admits that what he knows of Manson's lyrics and performances disturbs him. However, he argues, students of his who have been fans of Manson or of similar performers typically grow up to be well-adjusted adults, evidencing no lasting negative repercussions from their affinity for violent music. Parents of children who listen to songs that feature violent lyrics and themes should not necessarily assume that their children will be irreparably damaged, Fitzpatrick concludes.

As you read, consider the following questions:

1. Why is it impossible to keep children from being exposed to objectionable music groups, according to Fitzpatrick?
2. What motivates some teenagers to publicly affirm their allegiance to certain music groups, in the author's opinion?
3. What advice does Fitzpatrick give to parents whose teenagers listen to violent music?

I have never heard a song by this "Marilyn Manson" character. But I have read the horror stories about his "concerts"— about the salaciousness, homosexuality, and anti-Christian scatology that are central to his performances. His choice of a stage name that links the images of Marilyn Monroe and Charles Manson speaks volumes.

WHAT SHOULD PARENTS DO?

Many Christian parents are seeking some way to minimize his influence on their children, and I have no intention of calling for less vigilance. There is no place for this "music" in a Christian home. Do try to keep your kids away from it!

But what if you can't? Certain children who want to listen, will. There are too many places—car stereos, portable cassette players, and the like—for them to gain access. It is not like the days when most homes had just one hi-fi in the family room.

What should parents do if they think their children have become part of the Marilyn Manson audience? How much of a family confrontation is in order? Are there cases when parents can ride through this phenomenon, look the other way and hope for the best?

If your kids are experimenting with behaviors advocated by this lowlife, then drastic, confrontational measures may be necessary. But if your kids are living what seem to be otherwise moral and balanced lives, there may be no reason to be terribly alarmed.

What if their grades are okay, they are working part-time jobs, and seem to be basically "good kids" who are not displaying any harmful effects? Actually, many "good kids" listen to shock rock. I submit that there is a certain type of teenager who yearns to be openly associated with music that outrages responsible adults. More to the point, I hold that many of these kids go on to become sensible and productive adults, even practicing Christians. Your children may be in that category.

EXPERIENCES WITH STUDENTS

I have some experience in this area. I have been teaching high school students, in Catholic and public high schools, for over 30 years now, and I have seen the Elvis and Beatle wannabes, the would-be hippies and greasers, the Deadheads and head-bangers, the heavy-metal aficionados and acid rock fans, and the partisans of grunge, gangsta rap, alternative rock—you name it. I have learned little about the music itself—I don't listen to it—but I have learned about the kinds of kids who are drawn to it.

About 10 years ago a student of mine was going through a period when heavy-metal rock seemed to be the defining element of his life. He wore a "Metallica" T-shirt to my classes every day (it seemed) for the entire year. He even became involved in a minor confrontation with our pastor. He and his friends had formed a rock group and wanted to perform their heavy-metal songs at a dance in the church auditorium. The pastor, who knew nothing about the music, agreed—until a group of parents showed him the lyrics to some heavy-metal songs. No dance after all.

A series of letters to the editor in the local newspaper followed. Some parents complained that the parish gave much time and attention to teenage athletes and Irish step-dancers and participants in science fairs—the more mainstream kids—but was turning its back on the heavy-metal fans, who were, the parents insisted, just going through a harmless teenage enthusiasm. Others agreed with the pastor: that, whether the teenagers were decent kids or not, a church auditorium was no place for music associated with sinister hostility to Christian values.

I was on the pastor's side. But that is neither here nor there. What is of interest is that the boy in question, now a man in his late 20s, can be found a few rows in front of me with his mother at Mass on many Sundays. With his neat hair and white shirt, he could be the salesman in a computer ad.

I have seen fans of the other rock groups that caused great anxiety to parents in the 1980s—Ozzy Osbourne, Motley Crüe, Black Sabbath—mature in a similar way. I see them in coat and tie driving to the commuter train, at work in neighborhood businesses and the trades, in the malls with their own kids in tow.

Was the "music" beneficial for them? It would be silly to say so. No doubt it would have been better for them and their families if they had never been in that orbit. Yet whatever spiritual damage they suffered does not seem to have been lasting, at least from my decidedly unscientific survey. These kids went on to become young adults not noticeably different from those who were listening to the more mainstream rock music of the time. (I know of some kids who were Billy Joel fans who ended up with lives in turmoil.)

TEEN IDENTITY

I don't know why teenagers need to profess a tribal identity of some sort. No doubt the psychologists have a name for the phenomenon. But young people do. They go through that stage when their hair, clothes, T-shirt slogans, the cars they prefer—

and especially the rock groups they favor—are chosen as badges, uniforms, as a way of instantly proclaiming a persona that identifies them to every other teenager they pass. The establishment-oriented kids do it, too. They affect the preppy look. You can see it at every high school debate tournament—all those earnest young men in black overcoats and Hugh Grant batwing hairdos.

A Defense of Rap Music

Most attacks on rap music offer profoundly shallow readings of its use of violent and sexist imagery and rely on a handful of provocative and clearly troubling songs or lyrics. Rarely is the genre described in ways that encompass the range of passionate, horrifying, and powerful storytelling in rap and gangsta rap. Few critics in the popular realm . . . have responded to rap's disturbing elements in a way that attempts to understand the logic and motivations behind these facets of its expressions. . . .

Rap music has become a lightning rod for those politicians and law and order officials who are hell-bent on scapegoating it as a major source of violence instead of attending to the much more difficult and complicated work of transforming the brutally unjust institutions that shape the lives of poor people. Attacking rap during this so-called crisis of crime and violence is a facile smokescreen that protects the real culprits and deludes the public into believing that public officials are taking a bite out of crime. In the face of daunting economic and social conditions that are felt most severely by the young people they represent, rappers are cast as the perpetrators.

Tricia Rose, *USA Today*, May 1994.

The kids who publicly affirm their interest in the shock groups like Marilyn Manson tend to fall into a definable category. They are not usually outstanding scholars, athletes, or leaders of the school government. They usually do not have enough money to own a hot car. They are seldom ladies' men. Consequently, they are not on the receiving end of much adulation, either from other teenagers or from adults. Shock rock lends a certain cachet—in their eyes, at any rate—to this outsider status. They're trying to be outlaws rather than nerds, rebels instead of nobodies.

I would go so far as to argue that associating themselves with Marilyn Manson can be comparable—in their minds—to what Tom Sawyer was doing when he smoked his pipe and waved a dead rat in front of Becky Thatcher. It establishes rank as one of the hard guys, as an "I don't give a damn" type, a cynic who "takes no bull from the grownups," who has "guts" (although they use another part of the anatomy to make that point these days), who is not a jerk, no matter what the honor roll students, the jocks, and the principal think.

This point was driven home to me as I was walking around the gym while proctoring the final exams at my school. A scattering of kids was wearing the popular Marilyn Manson shirt emblazoned with "We Love Hate; We Hate Love," or some other Manson paraphernalia.

I couldn't help but notice: These kids were not the kids who have been arrested for selling drugs in school. They were not the kids who cause confrontations in the classroom. I noticed no tattoos, and about the "normal" level of body-piercing. They were not gang members. Many of them were kids who were also into computer games, or members of the school orchestra. One had his skateboard next to his desk. I'm serious! And I don't think my school is an anomaly.

MARILYN MANSON IS NOT THE ISSUE

Certainly, I wish they were not caught up in the Manson phenomenon. And I am not saying that what Manson advocates is in the same league as Tom Sawyer's pranks. Manson's act is vile. What is at issue, though, is not as much Manson as the students' perception of him. I am arguing that their public association with him is meant to accomplish for them what Tom Sawyer's bravado did for him. For the same reason, an adolescent boy will wave a frog or a snake in the playground, hang from the overpass to paint a graffito, throw snowballs at the principal's car. It's a form of derring-do which induces a frisson in the teenybopper girls—or so he hopes.

That's why the T-shirts with slogans are so essential in this scenario. They are advertisements proclaiming a defiance of authority—by young people who have not succeeded in making that point about themselves in other ways. They are not necessarily bad kids. But they want to be at least a little bit bad in the eyes of their peers. Nothing admirable about that; nothing heroic; but nothing all that out of place for a teenager either.

There is nothing easy about raising a Christian kid these days. The entertainment industry is pounding away at everything we hold sacred. Dealing with this latest wave of shock rock will test the mettle of those parents who are confronted with it. It is an indecency that must be fought. But it must be fought with weapons appropriate to the kid and the situation, and with a sense of proportion, lest we do more harm than good. "Fathers, do not nag your children, lest they lose heart," St. Paul advised the Colossians.

So be ready for the worst if you find your kids listening to Marilyn Manson, but don't jump to conclusions. My experience leads me to believe that it might not be the beginning of a deterioration in their character that will end in depravity. By this time next year, that Manson creep could very well be a forgotten episode in their lives—and yours.

PERIODICAL BIBLIOGRAPHY

The following articles have been selected to supplement the diverse views presented in this chapter. Addresses are provided for periodicals not indexed in the *Readers' Guide to Periodical Literature*, the *Alternative Press Index*, the *Social Sciences Index*, or the *Index to Legal Periodicals and Books*.

Charles Anderson	"Violence in Television Commercials During Nonviolent Programming," *JAMA*, October 1, 1997. Available from 515 N. State St., Chicago, IL 60610.
Alison Bell	"The Fear Factor," *Teen*, April 1997.
Brandon S. Centerwall	"Our Cultural Perplexities (V): Television and Violent Crime," *Public Interest*, Spring 1993.
Richard B. Felson	"Mass Media Effects on Violent Behavior," *Annual Review of Sociology*, vol. 22, 1996.
Jib Fowles	"The Violence Against Television Violence," *Television Quarterly*, vol. 28, no. 1, 1996.
Todd Gitlin	"Imagebusters: The Hollow Crusade Against TV Violence," *American Prospect*, Winter 1994.
Gloria Goodale	"Battles over Media Violence Move to a New Frontier: The Internet," *Christian Science Monitor*, November 18, 1996.
Mary A. Hepburn	"T.V. Violence: A Medium's Effects Under Scrutiny," *Social Education*, September 1997. Available from National Council for the Social Studies, 3501 Newark St. NW, Washington, DC 20016.
Jay Kist	"Does TV Affect Your Psyche?" *Current Health 2*, December 1996.
Richard Lacayo	"Violent Reaction," *Time*, June 12, 1995.
John Leland	"Violence, Reel to Real," *Newsweek*, December 11, 1995.
S. Robert Lichter	"Bam! Whoosh! Crack! TV Worth Squelching," *Insight*, December 19, 1994. Available from 21 Congress St., Salem, MA 01970.
Mike Males	"Stop Blaming Kids and TV," *Progressive*, October 1997.

Lawrie Mifflin	"Study Finds a Decline in TV Network Violence," *New York Times,* January 14, 1998.
Laura Outerbridge	"TV's Lesson: Kick First, Talk Later," *Insight,* March 25, 1996.
Joe Queenan	"Get a Grip, Guys: Violence Against Women," *TV Guide,* March 15–21, 1997.
Scott Stossel	"The Man Who Counts the Killings," *Atlantic Monthly,* May 1997.
Mortimer B. Zuckerman	"Forest Gump vs. Ice-T," *U.S. News & World Report,* July 24, 1995.

CHAPTER 2

SHOULD THE GOVERNMENT RESTRICT MEDIA VIOLENCE?

CHAPTER PREFACE

The power of the American government to regulate media violence is constrained by the First Amendment to the U.S. Constitution, which states that "Congress shall make no law . . . abridging the freedom of speech, or of the press." Laws restricting media violence have been successfully challenged in court. For example, a federal district court in 1992 ruled in the case of *Video Software Dealers Association v. Webster* that a Missouri statute banning the distribution of violent videos to minors was unconstitutional.

Television has been granted less First Amendment protection from government regulation than have most other forms of media because the electromagnetic spectrum over which television programs are broadcast is considered public property. Local television stations are given free use of the airwaves by obtaining licenses from the Federal Communications Commission (FCC) on the condition that they serve "the public interest, convenience, and necessity."

In exercising its powers to grant, withhold, renew, and revoke operating licenses, the FCC's primary concern is to prevent broadcast signals from interfering with each other. From time to time, however, both Congress and the FCC have passed laws and regulations that require television stations to meet certain programming conditions in order to maintain their operating licenses. These standards include restrictions on indecent material, a ban on cigarette advertising, and requirements mandating a minimum number of hours of children's educational programming.

Some members of Congress have proposed similar rules regulating or limiting the amount of television violence as a condition for license renewal; such restrictions, they argue, would serve the public interest. In 1996, Congress passed a law requiring that, within a few years, all new television sets would need to be equipped with a "V-chip"—a computer chip that enables parents to block out violent or sexually explicit programming. However, many critics believe that the V-chip law and other proposed regulations violate the First Amendment by giving the government too much control over television content. The viewpoints in the following chapter examine the various controversies surrounding the V-chip and other government restrictions of media violence.

"*As [television] industry defensiveness
. . . has increased, so has parental
pressure to use legislative vehicles in
forcing the industry to reduce violent
programming.*"

GOVERNMENT REGULATIONS RESTRICTING MEDIA VIOLENCE MAY BE NECESSARY

Helen K. Liebowitz

The Parent-Teacher Association (PTA) is a volunteer association that works to improve the education and welfare of America's children. The following viewpoint is taken from testimony presented before Congress in 1997 by Helen K. Liebowitz, a member of the National PTA Board of Directors. Liebowitz states that the PTA supports federal legislation designed to limit children's exposure to television violence. Such government action, she maintains, does not necessarily constitute censorship, which the PTA opposes. She argues that self-regulation by the television industry would be ideal, but the industry has not been responsive to parents' concerns. Stricter government laws curtailing violent content on television during times when children are most likely to be watching may become necessary if high levels of television violence continue to be transmitted into America's homes, she concludes.

As you read, consider the following questions:

1. What do parents want from the television industry, according to Liebowitz?
2. What rules governing television violence does Liebowitz suggest television broadcasters to adopt?

Reprinted from Helen K. Liebowitz's testimony in *Government and Television: Improving Programming Without Censorship*, a hearing before the U.S. Senate Subcommittee on Oversight of Government Management, Restructuring, and the District of Columbia, April 16, 1997.

M r. Chairman and members of the Senate Subcommittee on Oversight of Government Management, Restructuring and the District of Columbia. I am Helen K. Liebowitz, National PTA Health and Welfare Commission member and Team Leader for the National PTA's Critical Viewing Media Literacy Project. The National PTA is comprised of over 6.5 million parents, teachers, and other child advocates concerned about improving the quality of television programming for children. Thank you for this opportunity to present the views of many parents nationwide who have been frequently frustrated in their attempts to influence children's television programming while not wishing to cross the fine lines of First Amendment freedoms.

RIGHTS AND RESPONSIBILITIES

It is appropriate that you entitle this hearing: "Government and Television: Improving Programming Without Censorship." For the many years the National PTA has testified before Congress related to improving children's TV, we have *always* noted that the danger in industry resistance to providing better programming could be a national inclination toward outright program censorship. First Amendment rights can only be protected through responsibility. . . .

I come before this subcommittee not as a legal expert or a researcher, although this testimony incorporates facets of both legal opinion and research conclusions. As a parent, National PTA board member, former New York State PTA president, and a long standing activist in various community organizations, I do represent many parents and local citizens who are concerned about the influence of violent television programming on their children and family. Indeed, for some children, television acts as a surrogate parent. With a TV in 96% of all American households, TV obviously has a major effect on the attitudes, education, and behavior of our children.

The industry maintains that parents have the option of shutting off the TV if they don't like the programming. However, on the other hand, parents can't choose good programming if it is not available and they want to watch it. What parents are seeking, in an age when violence and children killing children and concerns about safety and character building are on the top of the national agenda, is a television industry that is responsive to their concerns. . . .

While we recognize the responsibility of parents to monitor what their children watch, the National PTA has always maintained that parents need assistance from the television industry, which more often than not, has turned a deaf ear to many parental requests for more excellent programming. Frequently, the industry has fought against any federal regulation which would require them to meet their obligation to the children's interest and, at the same time, resisted the option for voluntary self-regulation at improving television programs for children through the TV Violence Act. Cries of censorship, denial of freedom of the press, severe economic burden, and unconscionable meddling "by those national organizations who do not represent real parents" have all been justifications by the industry to maintain the status quo.

In fact, real parents flooded the Federal Communications Commission (FCC) with comments during the recent comment period related to the v-chip [a device that blocks television programming]. The following are excerpts from what some of the "real" parents had to say:

> I am not pleased with the language and situations which dominate many of the television shows which are on the air today. My first preference would be to eliminate the material, but as that does not seem likely in the near future, I feel the very least that can be done for families is to allow intelligent decisions.

> Janet E. Boatman, Kingman, Texas PTA

> My husband and I both feel there is too much sex, violence and trash on the TV and find it difficult to find programs that are suitable for the whole family to watch together.

> Mr. and Mrs. R.T. Varkalis, Montgomery County, Maryland PTA

> To give you an example, I have five year old twins and an eight year old. My eight year old is much more easily disturbed by violence on television than are either of my younger children.

> Barbara C. Coe, Glen Haven Elementary School PTA, Silver Spring, Maryland ...

We want the TV industry to understand that in many households, children may be watching television unsupervised with no adult to make program choices. With the increasing number of latchkey children and working families, this situation is becoming a fact of life. Parents are not asking for censorship; they are asking the industry for a little assistance. Clearly this committee would not protect teachers who taught violence to children. Yet why would we condone a steady diet of children being exposed to TV violence, year after year? The Nielson Index estimates that the average child will have witnessed some 18,000 murders and countless robberies, bombings, smugglings, assaults and beatings during their years of TV viewing. What kind of social role-modeling is that for children to emulate? How is it possible that this program menu could be educationally redeeming or have any positive impact on the character of our youth?

TELEVISION VIOLENCE

From our members, we have learned that there are few single issues that preoccupy parents more than the poor quality of children's television that many believe contribute to a violent society. The statistics related to a child's exposure to television violence are indeed alarming. The numerous studies that link watching television violence to aggressive behavior in children are well known in the policy making and regulatory realms.

Particularly disturbing to our members are findings of research studies which show three possible effects of viewing television violence on young people. According to Rand researchers John P. Murray and Barbara Lonnberg, television violence can create the following effects:

- Children may become less sensitive to the pain and suffering of others;
- they may be more fearful of the world around them; and
- they may be more likely to behave in an aggressive or harmful way toward others.

According to several recent studies, television violence has not diminished, despite the passage of the 1990 Television Violence Act, the Children's Television Act, and the v-chip provision in the Telecommunications Act. A March 1997 study concluded that there has been no meaningful change in the presentation of violence on television between 1994 and 1996. The National Television Violence Study conducted by the University of California, Santa Barbara, found little change in such elements as the portrayal of pain and harm to victims or the long-term negative consequences that result from violence from 1994–1995 and 1995–1996. The researchers identified over 18,000 violent incidents in a sample of more than 2,000 hours drawn from 23 cable and broadcast channels during the 1995–1996 television season. Over half of all the violent incidents still failed to show the victim suffering any pain. Long-term negative consequences from violence were portrayed in only 16% of the programs. . . . In addition, three out of four violent scenes contained no remorse, criticism, or penalty for violence, and "bad" characters go unpunished in 37% of the programs. Television programs that employed a strong anti-violence theme remained extremely rare, holding constant at 4% of all violent shows.

Many parents are beginning to complain, not only about violent program content, but also about violence in promos and advertisements as well. A 1996 UCLA report on this issue defined television promos as video highlights to sell a product of the network and to expose viewers to new programs. The report said that promos raise serious concerns, particularly because they feature violence out of context. It is almost impossible, says the report, to provide sufficient context for any violence that does occur. The study concludes that violence is used in many ways in promos as a "hook" to draw viewers into the programs.

BALANCING PARENTS' NEEDS AND THE FIRST AMENDMENT

In light of this research and little change in the reduction in TV violence, the National PTA has been vigilant and responsible in attempting to balance the needs of parents and children with the requirements of the First Amendment freedom of speech. Our preference has always been to seek non-legislative solutions to children's television issues, but as industry defensiveness and resistance to parental concerns about violence on television has increased, so has parental pressure to use legislative vehicles in forcing the industry to reduce violent programming and increase educational options for families. In fact, parents have been extremely patient with the industry and have accepted some of the responsibility in choosing television programs for their families.

While the National PTA is concerned about issues of censorship, let us be clear that we do not equate government action in the telecommunications area with censorship. The combination of purposeful Congressional policies and voluntary industry efforts are essential as we discuss a telecommunications framework that will work for children and creative artists alike. In addition, there is no single quick fix to better television, no panacea that will eliminate TV violence overnight. But the greater industry resistance is to change, the greater Congressional action will be to pressure them to do so.

For instance, the National Cable Television Association with Cable in the Classroom has been working with the National PTA over the past several years in the Family and Community Critical Viewing Skills project. This cooperative effort is designed to provide parents and teachers throughout the community with information and skills to help families make better choices in the television programs they watch, and to improve the way they watch these programs. We are tremendously proud of this project and relationship. To complement this project with a reduction in TV violence, the meaningful implementation of the Children's Television Act and descriptive content-based ratings and industry voluntary self-regulation would be ideal.

Unfortunately, the other piece to this equation—reduction of violence—has not occurred, and parents do not want to shoulder the full burden of responsibility for making sure their children do not watch violent TV without some help from the industry. In other words, parents do not and should not shoulder the full responsibility for television they never asked for, do not want, and they are tired of being patient. . . .

Toles. Copyright ©1994 The Buffalo News. Reprinted by permission of Universal Press Syndicate. All rights reserved.

Senators Sam Brownbeck and Joseph Lieberman, you now ask whether the National PTA would support S. 471, the Television Improvement Act of 1997, to allow broadcasters, free from antitrust restrictions, to once again come together to develop a National Broadcasters Code of Conduct. . . . This proposed law is similar to the Television Violence Act of 1990 that the industry basically squandered away in blatant disregard for Congress and parents.

We testified in support of the Television Violence Act and will support this similar measure. In the absence of antitrust laws, the broadcasters could come together without legal impunity.

S. 471 removes the legal consequences that might otherwise be barriers as the broadcasters take action to address TV violence. The problem is that the bill does not compel the broadcasters to agree or to implement anything. . . .

The National PTA has vivid recollections of how the industry failed to take advantage of the last antitrust exemption they received as a result of the Children's Violence Act of 1990. While that bill had a three-year sunset, it did provide adequate time for the broadcasters to meet and agree on a National Code, but they never did. As each of these efforts fail, I can tell this committee that this nation comes ever closer to the day when the American people will demand that Congress take arbitrary action to curtail TV violence, if voluntary action once again fails.

GOOD PUBLIC RELATIONS

If I were the industry, just imagine the good public relations the broadcasters could create around a Code that includes:

- Special recognition for programs that are violent-free
- Identification of sponsors that do not sponsor violent programming or violent commercials
- When violence is presented, provide greater emphasis on a strong anti-violence theme
- Broadcast anti-violence public service announcements focusing on such events as gang membership, alternatives to violent behavior, and address behavior that can lead to violence
- Make commitments to identify all programming that is educational as well as programming that is violent

However, waiting in the Congressional wings is "safe harbor" legislation [that would strictly regulate television content of designated hours] which the National PTA will support as a last resort in the event the industry is incapable of reducing violent programming. Parents want safe schools and safe communities.

Safety is not a Republican issue or a Democratic issue; it not an issue of the South or North; and it is not an issue of men or women. Should it happen that these groups converge their energies and power on an industry that continues to ignore public opinion, the industry risks losing those same freedoms which up to this time it has touted in its defense. Ultimately, the airwaves belong to the public and there just may be a time when the public wishes to take them back.

"*Viewing decisions can, and should, be made at home, without government interference.*"

GOVERNMENT REGULATION OF MEDIA VIOLENCE IS UNCONSTITUTIONAL CENSORSHIP

American Civil Liberties Union

The following viewpoint is excerpted from a position paper on freedom of expression by the American Civil Liberties Union (ACLU), the nation's oldest and largest civil liberties organization. The ACLU argues that the First Amendment guarantees of free speech and freedom of the press apply to the creation of motion pictures, television shows, music lyrics, and other forms of art and entertainment. Government laws aimed at regulating media content, such as efforts to restrict television violence, constitute unconstitutional censorship, according to the ACLU. Freedom of expression should be restricted only when it would cause an immediate public danger (such as by shouting "fire" in a crowded theater), the organization maintains, and television violence has not been proven to pose such a danger to the American people.

As you read, consider the following questions:

1. How have Americans historically felt about government censorship, according to the ACLU?
2. What have studies established about the relationship between real violence and media violence, according to the ACLU?
3. According to the ACLU, what fundamental belief is the First Amendment based upon?

Reprinted from American Civil Liberties Union, "Freedom of Expression in the Arts and Entertainment," *ACLU Briefing Paper*, no. 14, ©1997 American Civil Liberties Union.

In the late 1980s, state prosecutors brought a criminal obscenity charge against the owner of a record store for selling an album by the rap group, 2 Live Crew. Although this was the first time that obscenity charges had ever been brought against song lyrics, the 2 Live Crew case focused the nation's attention on an old question: should the government ever have the authority to dictate to its citizens what they may or may not listen to, read, or watch?

AMERICAN AMBIVALENCE

American society has always been deeply ambivalent about this question. On the one hand, our history is filled with examples of overt government censorship, from the 1873 Comstock Law to the 1996 Communications Decency Act. Anthony Comstock, head of the Society for the Suppression of Vice, boasted 194,000 "questionable pictures" and 134,000 pounds of books of "improper character" were destroyed under the Comstock Law—in the first year alone. The Communications Decency Act imposed an unconstitutional censorship scheme on the Internet, accurately described by a federal judge as "the most participatory form of mass speech yet developed."

On the other hand, the commitment to freedom of imagination and expression is deeply embedded in our national psyche, buttressed by the First Amendment, and supported by a long line of Supreme Court decisions.

Provocative and controversial art and in-your-face entertainment put our commitment to free speech to the test. Why should we oppose censorship when scenes of murder and mayhem dominate the TV screen, when works of art can be seen as a direct insult to peoples' religious beliefs, and when much sexually explicit material can be seen as degrading to women? Why not let the majority's morality and taste dictate what others can look at or listen to?

The answer is simple, and timeless: a free society is based on the principle that each and every individual has the right to decide what art or entertainment he or she wants—or does not want—to receive or create. Once you allow the government to censor someone else, you cede to it the power to censor you, or something you like. Censorship is like poison gas: a powerful weapon that can harm you when the wind shifts.

Freedom of expression for ourselves requires freedom of expression for others. It is at the very heart of our democracy. . . .

Today's calls for censorship are not motivated solely by morality and taste, but also by the widespread belief that exposure to images of violence *causes* people to act in destructive ways. Pro-censorship forces, including many politicians, often cite a multitude of "scientific studies" that allegedly prove fictional violence leads to real-life violence.

There is, in fact, virtually no evidence that fictional violence causes otherwise stable people to become violent. And if we suppressed material based on the actions of unstable people, no work of fiction or art would be safe from censorship. Serial killer Theodore Bundy collected cheerleading magazines. And the work most often cited by psychopaths as justification for their acts of violence is the Bible.

But what about the rest of us? Does exposure to media violence actually lead to criminal or anti-social conduct by otherwise stable people, including children, who spend an average of 28 hours watching television each week? These are important questions. If there really were a clear cause-and-effect relationship between what normal children see on TV and harmful actions, then limits on such expression might arguably be warranted.

WHAT THE STUDIES SHOW

Studies on the relationship between media violence and real violence are the subject of considerable debate. Children have been shown TV programs with violent episodes in a laboratory setting and then tested for "aggressive" behavior. Some of these studies suggest that watching TV violence may temporarily induce "object aggression" in some children (such as popping balloons or hitting dolls or playing sports more aggressively) but not actual criminal violence against another person.

Correlational studies that seek to explain why some aggressive people have a history of watching a lot of violent TV suffer from the chicken-and-egg dilemma: does violent TV cause such people to behave aggressively, or do aggressive people simply prefer more violent entertainment? There is no definitive answer. But all scientists agree that statistical correlations between two phenomena do not mean that one causes the other.

International comparisons are no more helpful. Japanese TV and movies are famous for their extreme, graphic violence, but Japan has a very low crime rate—much lower than many societies in which television watching is relatively rare. What the studies reveal on the issue of fictional violence and real world aggression is—not much.

The only clear assertion that can be made is that the relationship between art and human behavior is a very complex one. Violent and sexually explicit art and entertainment have been a staple of human cultures from time immemorial. Many human behavioralists believe that these themes have a useful and constructive societal role, serving as a vicarious outlet for individual aggression.

The First Amendment

The Supreme Court has interpreted the First Amendment's protection of artistic expression very broadly. It extends not only to books, theatrical works and paintings, but also to posters, television, music videos and comic books—whatever the human creative impulse produces.

Two fundamental principles come into play whenever a court must decide a case involving freedom of expression. The first is "content neutrality"—the government cannot limit expression just because any listener, or even the majority of a community, is offended by its content. In the context of art and entertainment, this means tolerating some works that we might find offensive, insulting, outrageous—or just plain bad.

The second principle is that expression may be restricted only if it will clearly cause *direct and imminent* harm to an important societal interest. The classic example is falsely shouting fire in a crowded theater and causing a stampede. Even then, the speech may be silenced or punished only if there is no other way to avert the harm.

Blaming the Media

Whatever influence fictional violence has on behavior, most experts believe its effects are marginal compared to other factors. Even small children know the difference between fiction and reality, and their attitudes and behavior are shaped more by their life circumstances than by the books they read or the TV they watch. In 1972, the U.S. Surgeon General's Advisory Committee on Television and Social Behavior released a 200-page report, *Television and Growing Up: The Impact of Televised Violence*, which concluded, "The effect [of television] is small compared with many other possible causes, such as parental attitudes or knowledge of and experience with the real violence of our society." Twenty-one years later, the American Psychological Association published its 1993 report, *Violence & Youth*, and concluded, "The greatest predictor of future violent behavior is a previous history of violence." In 1995, the Center for Communication Policy at UCLA, which monitors TV violence, came to a similar conclusion in its yearly report: "It is known that television does not have a simple, direct stimulus-response effect on its audiences."

Blaming the media does not get us very far, and, to the extent that diverts the public's attention from the real causes of violence in society, it may do more harm than good.

BROADCASTERS' FIRST AMENDMENT RIGHTS

Several unpersuasive arguments have been presented as to why broadcasters should not get full free speech rights. First, it is argued that broadcasters use public property. But so do speakers in public parks, and so do newspapers, which are delivered through the public streets and printed on paper made from trees that grew on federal lands. Furthermore, there is no sound reason that the electromagnetic spectrum should have been seized by the government. Government ownership of the spectrum is inefficient and unnecessary. . . .

Some also claim that broadcasters cannot enjoy full First Amendment rights because broadcasting is too powerful and too pervasive to be free. But broadcasters are hardly more powerful than newspapers were in the 19th and early 20th century. And broadcasting faces competition from a growing number of other media outlets, from cable television to Direct Broadcast Satellites, the Internet, movies, VCRs, and, as always, the print media. Furthermore, television and radio are pervasive only when we want them to be; nobody is forced to own a radio or television set, or to turn it on. Finally, *if we fear the power and pervasiveness of broadcasting, we should especially fear the power of government control of broadcasting*. . . .

Most of the restrictions on broadcast speech have been ostensibly imposed to protect children. But we do not help children by letting parents think that the government can substitute for supervised television viewing. We can best set an example for children by showing them that the First Amendment is much more than a bothersome obstacle to government, to be gotten around by indirect threats and economic pressure.

Cato Handbook for Congress: 105th Congress, 1997.

A pro-censorship member of Congress once attacked the following shows for being too violent: *The Miracle Worker, Civil War Journal, Star Trek Deep Space 9, The Untouchables,* and *Teenage Mutant Ninja Turtles*. What would be left if all these kinds of programs were purged from the airwaves? Is there good violence and bad violence? If so, who decides? Sports and the news are at least as violent as fiction, from the fights that erupt during every televised hockey game, to the videotaped beating of Rodney King by the LA Police Department, shown over and over again on prime time TV. If we accept censorship of violence in the media, we will have to censor sports and news programs.

INDIVIDUAL RIGHTS, INDIVIDUAL DECISIONS

The First Amendment is based upon the belief that in a free and democratic society, individual adults must be free to decide for themselves what to read, write, paint, draw, see and hear. If we are disturbed by images of violence or sex, we can change the channel, turn off the TV, and decline to go to certain movies or museum exhibits.

We can also exercise our own free speech rights by voicing our objections to forms of expression that we don't like. Justice Louis Brandeis' advice that the remedy for messages we disagree with or dislike in art, entertainment or politics is "more speech, not enforced silence," is as true today as it was when given in 1927.

Further, we can exercise our prerogative as parents without resorting to censorship. Devices now exist that make it possible to block access to specific TV programs and internet sites. Periodicals that review books, recordings, and films can help parents determine what they feel is appropriate for their youngsters. Viewing decisions can, and should, be made at home, without government interference.

"This technology offers some real tangible benefits to parents who are concerned about the impact of TV violence . . . on their children."

THE V-CHIP CAN REDUCE CHILDREN'S EXPOSURE TO TELEVISION VIOLENCE

Dick Rolfe

Dick Rolfe is the president of the Dove Foundation, a nonprofit organization that promotes the creation of movies and TV programs suitable for children and produces film ratings and guides for families. He also writes a regular monthly column called "Hollywood and the Family." The following viewpoint is excerpted from two of his columns. Rolfe argues that the "V-chip" —computer technology that would enable television sets to block specially coded broadcast programming—can be used by parents to prevent their children from viewing violent or otherwise inappropriate television programs. He urges Congress to pass legislation that would require the V-chip to be installed in all new television sets. (Congress passed such legislation in February 1996, mandating the installation of V-chips in new television sets within a few years.)

As you read, consider the following questions:

1. What economic impact might the V-chip have on the television networks, according to Rolfe?
2. What does Rolfe consider to be the V-chip's most outstanding feature?
3. How does the American public feel about the V-chip, according to the author?

Reprinted from Dick Rolfe, "The V-Chip Controversy" and "The V-Chip Controversy Rages On," Hollywood and the Family column, August and September 1995, respectively, at www.dove.org/frames/column.htm, by permission of the author.

I

If you're shopping for a new TV set, but like most parents, you feel overwhelmed by all the violence, sex and raw language on television, hang in there. Help is on its way.

Coming to a television near you . . . a new technology that promises to help parents parent more effectively. It's called the "v-chip." V is for violence. This little silicone wafer will probably be installed in every newly manufactured television set sold in America very soon. It will allow viewers to block certain explicit programming from their homes by punching a few buttons on their remote control keypads.

V-Chip Legislation

Congress is proposing legislation to introduce this new technology in response to millions of complaints from virtually every segment of the marketplace about the abundance of sex, violence and profanity on television. This issue is not without controversy, however. Both sides of the political aisle agree that media has gone too far. The disparity between them is not how far, but in which direction. Violence seems to be the hot issue with Democrats, while explicit sex and profanity seems to offend Republicans more. Other differences between them center around their proposed solutions. The Dems are eager to regulate the situation, while the GOP would rather put pressure on the offenders and embarrass them into compliance. In either case, the Senate has already passed a v-chip bill and a House version is not far behind. [A v-chip mandate was signed into law in February 1996.]

The legislation will permit the entertainment industry ample time for self-regulation. Even though this is exactly what Hollywood petitioned for—the right to clean up their own backyard—they would rather be left alone to do it in their own time and their own way. The legislative caveat here is that if television programmers don't do the job themselves, Congress will have the power to appoint an independent panel to set the standards for them.

It's not going to be easy getting network and cable executives to define, much less label, program content that falls into the category of "violence, nudity and other objectionable material."

Unlike the subtle "Parental Advisory" label, this new alternative will actually activate a device in millions of households that will measurably shrink the audience of adult-themed programs. This will result in the targeted programs being of less value to advertisers, and therefore less profitable to the networks.

Real Benefits

Nothing is perfect. But this technology offers some real tangible benefits to parents who are concerned about the impact of TV violence and sexual content on their children. One advantage is that it will replace the need for mom or dad to resort to more drastic means of controlling their kid's viewing habits, like hiding the TV power cord, or locking the set in the closet. And the v-chip works. It was successfully tested in Canada in 1994. Manufacturers say it will add only about $5 to the retail price of a television set. It is simple to operate—sort of a programmable, content-sensitive "on/off" switch. The "on" option should silence cries of "censorship."

"Now that we've had a chip installed that blocks out violent shows, there really ISN'T anything on TV!"

Bruce Beattie. Reprinted by permission of Copley News Service.

I'm opposed to a lot of government interference in our society. However, the v-chip seems to be the most practical solution, short of intervention, that has been suggested thus far. Its most outstanding feature is that it empowers parents to do their jobs more effectively. Those opposed to this option have not offered any alternative suggestions.

II

Since my last column, "The V-Chip Controversy," the battle lines are being drawn. Here is a look at the public's response to this high tech "on/off" switch. A poll of 1010 adults was commissioned by The Hollywood Reporter. It found that the American public is overwhelming in favor of the V-Chip technology which prohibits violent or sexually explicit programming from being shown on a TV set, by a whopping 82%. And 72% said they would use the V-Chip if it were in their TV sets at home. Furthermore, 78% felt that "violence depicted in movies and music contributes [somewhat, or a lot] to crime in America." 79% either strongly or somewhat "agree with the politicians' assertion that the entertainment industry is accountable for putting profits ahead of 'common decency.'"

CONSERVATIVE OPPOSITION

One would assume that with such popular support, there would be little opposition to the V-Chip. But there is. And it's from the conservatives who are worried about too much government intervention. The Media Research Center, a conservative watchdog organization with Rush Limbaugh on its advisory board, declares, "From a conservative perspective, mandating the installation of the chips is hardly a business-friendly measure. . . ." They proceed to quote only those notables who nix the proposition; from network executives (surprise) to Don Wildmon, President of the American Family Association, who said, the chip "sounds like a good step on the surface, but in the long run would absolve the entertainment industry of [its] responsibility." Conservative magazine The American Spectator prophesied, "There is not the slightest chance that broadcasters will, or can, develop a uniform rating code." They deduce that a "government committee would be sure to step in. Bureaucrats would apply their own standards to determine what is appropriate for the rest of us to watch."

INDUSTRIES CAN PRACTICE SELF-CONTROL

Those accounts sound ominous, assuming the prognosis is accurate. Time has shown that, given the proper government "incentive," any industry can practice the most amazing degree of self-control. Would you and I have seat belts to buckle if passenger safety had been left to car makers? Or, in a related issue, would there be Parental Advisory labels on television programs if politicians hadn't set deadlines for the television industry to self-regulate? Speaking of Parental Advisory labels, the broadcasters must already have a pretty good sense of what content is "too violent" for certain audiences. Otherwise, how would they know which programs to label?

On one hand, the conservatives are right. If the government

decides what content the V-Chip should block, that's censorship. If, on the other hand, the industry will knuckle down and do some radical soul searching about its program content, something good can happen. Programmers should consider changing their ways, not because of Congressional mandates, but in response to the public's outcry.

"There's no guarantee that . . . having a chip in every [television] set will solve anything."

THE V-CHIP IS AN INADEQUATE SAFEGUARD AGAINST TELEVISION VIOLENCE

Rob Sabey

In February 1996, President Bill Clinton signed a law that required new television sets to include a V-chip that would allow viewers to block out certain shows. The legislation also provided for the creation of a television rating system by either the television industry or the Federal Communications Commission (FCC). In the following viewpoint, Rob Sabey, a freelance writer, argues that these steps do not go far enough to prevent children from being exposed to violence and other objectionable material on television. The V-chip will not help children of irresponsible parents who will not use it or families who cannot afford to buy a new television set, he contends. Sabey concludes that society must make it illegal for television networks and stations to broadcast material that is too violent or in other ways unacceptable to most families.

As you read, consider the following questions:

1. What claims of President Clinton does Sabey disagree with?
2. What happened to motion pictures after a ratings system was introduced, according to Sabey?
3. What is society's purpose in creating laws, according to the author?

Reprinted from Rob Sabey, "V-Chips and Ratings Won't Help and May Hurt," *The Christian Science Monitor*, Opinion/Essays, March 12, 1996, by permission of the author.

President Bill Clinton hails the so-called V-chip and a TV-rating system as a step forward in the fight for traditional family values. He's wrong. If we continue on this course, we'll open the way to a moral decline in our society that will be worse than anything we've seen in this country's history.

FAULTY SUPPOSITIONS

Mr. Clinton claims that by providing a rating system, parents will be able to make educated decisions about what to allow their children to watch. Yet this presupposes that parents will accept the responsibility of monitoring their children's choice of shows. What about the children in families where parents don't care and don't take responsibility?

Children from these families are already a major social risk. These are the kids who too often join gangs and lead criminal and violent lives. These are the children who don't understand the consequences of their actions because their parents don't take the responsibility of teaching them.

These parents allow their children to rent R-rated videos or watch R-rated movies on cable. What makes us think they are going to be more responsible when it comes to TV shows?

The president's claim also presupposes that there will be a selection of shows or movies with different ratings to choose from. But consider what happened to the movie industry after ratings were introduced: Once Hollywood had license to create sexually explicit, violent, and/or vulgar movies, such films became the norm.

This is likely to happen in the broadcast and cable industries as well. We'll be offered a prime-time selection of R-rated sitcoms and dramas on network TV and will have to turn to the Learning Channel to find something the whole family can watch. TV ratings also will eliminate the need for "edited for TV" movies.

Too often it seems that violent, vulgar, or sexual content is added to a movie to get it a "more marketable" R rating. Movie-makers frequently claim that this content helps portray a more "realistic" picture. The fact remains, however, that countless Americans have made the choice that they will not view R-rated movies.

I, for one, look forward to seeing these movies in an edited form on TV. Because of the broadcast industry's higher moral standard, the sex, graphic violence, and vulgar profanities have been eliminated. If a TV-rating system is introduced, I will no longer be able to watch these movies because they will appear in their original unedited form.

V-Chip Limitations

Clinton also claims that the V-chip technology will allow us to "hand the remote back to parents." Wrong again. The technology will work only if 1) every TV in a particular household has the chip, and 2) parents take the responsibility to use it correctly.

That takes us back to the children who are caught up in a life of crime and violence precisely because their parents don't take responsibility. Will a V-chip or a rating system change that? Sadly, the answer is no.

What about those parents who *are* willing to take responsibility for what their children watch? Will the V-chip help them by providing an automated tool to cancel out inappropriate programming?

For the V-chip to work, families must replace their current sets, or perhaps purchase third-party boxes that attach to the cable or antenna input of the TV. This solution discriminates against the poor—most low-income families won't be able to afford the expense. It also creates undue hardship for middle-income families trying to save for college educations and retirement and pay their mortgages.

Borgman. Reprinted with special permission of King Features Syndicate.

Requiring families to replace their TV sets is unacceptable. Furthermore, there's no guarantee that even having a chip in every set will solve anything. VCRs don't have V-chips. What's to stop a child from taping a show and taking that tape to a friend's house where the TV is V-chipless? What's to stop a child from going to that friend's house and viewing the program to begin with?

A BETTER SOLUTION

The solution, then, is to make it illegal for networks and cable companies to broadcast sex, violence, and vulgarity in the first place. Laws are tangible evidences of the values of our society. If we as a society value traditional family morals, then our laws should reflect those values.

Opponents of such a solution will say it violates important freedoms. Yet I'm not suggesting we stop people from making violent, sexual, or vulgar movies. I believe in their right to do this. I do not, however, believe in their right to come into my home with their "free speech."

Society must create laws to protect its members from themselves and others. We outlaw drugs to protect ourselves from ourselves and one another. We outlaw prostitution to protect ourselves from ourselves. Movies and shows that contain sex, violence, and vulgarity are no less addictive. Let's stop the wholesale distribution of such programming by legislating against it.

"The benefits of the chip will be almost nil. The costs to our freedom are significant."

V-Chip Legislation Violates the First Amendment

Solveig Bernstein

In February 1996, President Bill Clinton signed a law requiring that within a few years new television sets should be equipped with a V-chip (technology that blocks out designated broadcast programming). The legislation also called for the creation of a ratings system to work in conjunction with the V-chip, to be devised by either the Federal Communications Commission (FCC) or by the television industry, subject to FCC approval. The age-based ratings system the television industry introduced on a trial basis in December 1996 was criticized by many for failing to include more information on the content of television programs; it was also the subject of congressional hearings in February 1997. In the following viewpoint, Solveig Bernstein (now Solveig Singleton) asserts that these congressional hearings demonstrate that the V-chip and television ratings provisions of the 1996 law open the door to government censorship of television and other media. Bernstein, director of information studies at the Cato Institute, a market-oriented libertarian think tank, argues that the V-chip and ratings legislation threaten First Amendment freedoms while failing to help the intended beneficiaries.

As you read, consider the following questions:

1. According to Bernstein, in what respects does the V-chip violate the First Amendment?
2. What kinds of measures are needed to truly act against violence, according to the author?

Reprinted from Solveig Bernstein, "V-Chipping Away at the First Amendment," *Cato This Just In*, February 26, 1997, at www.cato.org/dailys/2-26-97.html, by permission of the Cato Institute, Washington, D.C.

Congress is gearing up for hearings on the television rating system. Since Congress can not constitutionally directly regulate violence on television, we got the V-chip and a "voluntary" television rating system. What's wrong with this picture? When politicians scapegoat the media into "self-regulation," they make a mockery of the First Amendment. They mock the problem of violence, too, by pretending that public hearings on ratings can substitute for parental involvement and real social reform.

The V-chip is unlikely to be used in poor households with older televisions, which don't contain the chips, or in homes with neglected kids. It's most likely to be used by parents already committed to involvement in their children's education—that is, in homes where the children are at low risk for developing violent behavior.

Truly addressing the problem of violence means tackling welfare and education reform. But the debate over the adequacy of the rating system promises politicians endless opportunities to spout anti-violence rhetoric, and that, it seems, is more appealing than hard choices about absent fathers and schools that can't teach kids how to read.

COSTS TO OUR FREEDOM

So the benefits of the chip will be almost nil. The costs to our freedom are significant. Once the V-chip is in place, nothing stops government from using informal pressures to approve or disapprove ratings. Lawmakers could force ratings of a far different kind than those originally proposed. That should have been predicted but apparently was not. When the V-chip law was passed, the television industry stated that ratings would be "totally voluntary. There will be no government involvement of any kind. [G]overnment censorship . . . no matter how benign in its public declarations, is fundamentally in conflict with more than 200 years of . . . freedom of speech."

But already Congress is holding hearings to see if perhaps the rating system should include more information—or perhaps rate advertising, too. Some members of Congress favor something like the old Canadian rating system, which included separate ratings for profane language, sex, and violence, as well as age-based labels. Canadians shelved that system when parents found it too complicated.

The idea that politicians could pressure broadcasters to adopt one system rather than another is ominous. As the winds of politics shift, there's no reason for lawmakers to confine their attentions to sex, swearing, and violence. Perhaps V-chips will be used to block negative political advertising, alcohol ads, or diaper advertising. V-chips could be installed on the spines of books. After all, political and religious works, including the Bible and the Communist Manifesto, have given rise to far more violence than has television. And we can have V-chips in our computers, with a "voluntary" ratings system approved by Congressional hearings to ensure that we do not meet with any violence on the Internet.

FIRST AMENDMENT IMPLICATIONS

Many people have tuned out the First Amendment implications of the V-chip debate. They have concluded that there is an unacceptable level of violence on the small screen and that something must be done to protect children.

As a defender of the First Amendment, I see the V-chip as coming dangerously close to government censorship.

Solange E. Bitol, *Washington Times*, October 12, 1997.

The whole idea of the First Amendment is to protect the media from the political process. The V-chip combined with hearings about "voluntary" rating does away with those protections in an instant.

ALTERNATIVES TO THE V-CHIP

What if we had no V-chip? What are busy parents to do? Turn the television off, or sit down with their children on the weekend and explain which programs are off limits? If that common-sense solution is unreasonable, there's other technology. Around the time the V-chip law was enacted, a new industry was beginning to offer parents different blocking options. If there were significant demand for blocking technology, those devices could be developed further. Several rating systems could have competed to serve parents with different values and concerns. That solution was shouldered out of the way by the monopoly V-chip.

The V-chip plus hearings turn the art of informally harassing the press into a science. Congress can regulate the press without the bother of going to court, running a rating system by remote control. Maybe George Orwell had it right—the constitution can be defeated by a computer chip.

"The very invocation of the word, 'censorship' in this TV ratings debate is completely out of proportion and out of context."

V-CHIP LEGISLATION DOES NOT VIOLATE THE FIRST AMENDMENT

Edward Markey

Edward Markey was the primary congressional sponsor of the 1996 law that requires new television sets (within a few years of its enactment) to be equipped with V-chips—devices that can block out designated broadcasts. In the following viewpoint, Markey, a member of Congress representing Massachusetts, asserts that the law does not threaten to create a system of government censorship. The ratings system devised to work in conjunction with the V-chip was created by the television industry, not by the government, he argues, and simply provides a way of giving parents greater information and consumer choice. He contends that the V-chip simply empowers parents to control their children's television viewing. The legislation does not curtail the rights of television programmers to produce violent or sexual programming, Markey asserts, or the rights of adults to watch such programs. First Amendment freedoms thus are not threatened by the V-chip, he concludes.

As you read, consider the following questions:

1. Under the law, who makes the decisions regarding the television ratings system, according to Markey?
2. What does the author compare to a TV rating?
3. How many acts of violence will the average American child have seen on television by the time he or she leaves elementary school, according to Markey?

Reprinted from Edward Markey, "Tuned In . . . and Out on the V-Chip: Beneficial Technology," *The Washington Times*, October 12, 1997, by permission of Scripps-Howard News Service.

The TV industry has started redeeming its pledge to parents by providing information on the television screen about the content of upcoming television shows. "V" (for violence), for example, or "S" (for sexual material) are attached when appropriate to "PG" ("parental guidance suggested") or "TV-14."

With the help of this information, and the advent of the "V-chip" technology in TV sets in 1998, parents will have the option to use these ratings to block violent or sexually oriented programming from the TV screen when they are not in the room to supervise their children.

MISPLACED FEARS OF CENSORSHIP

The American Civil Liberties Union (ACLU) and some in the TV industry have been straining to find a violation of the First Amendment in this welcome development. I don't begrudge the ACLU's vigilance, but in this case its fears could not be more misplaced.

Indeed, the very invocation of the word, "censorship" in this TV ratings debate is completely out of proportion and out of context. "Censorship" is supposed to mean official attempts to control what you can see or hear. But the V-chip law doesn't require the TV industry to do any ratings. Its basic mandate falls not on the broadcasters and cable companies, but on the set manufacturers. It requires that the technology be built into TV sets, but it does not mandate the rating system.

Question: Under the law, who decides whether to rate a TV show? Answer: the TV industry, not the government. Who decides what the rating should be for a particular program? The TV industry, not the government. Who decides whether to use the ratings? Parents, not the government.

A TV rating simply tells the consumer what is in the product. It is akin to the label on a can of soup. While companies always attempt to knock out such labels on the charge of "censorship," the courts have, time and again, found such labels to be consistent with the First Amendment, even when the government has required the label and specified the words, the size, even the very placement of the label on the product. After all, giving people more information, not less, is one of the core values that the First Amendment seeks to protect.

EMPOWERING PARENTS

In fact, parents, not the government, will ultimately decide the value of this whole undertaking, and that is how it should be. The advance of technology has made it possible to provide the V-chip in every new TV set at minimum cost. This gives parents an opportunity to create a "safe harbor" for their children in their own living rooms, but the decision to use it or not is entirely theirs. The only Big Brother figures in this story are TV executives who refuse to concede any decision-making power to parents.

The Television Ratings System

TV Y Material suitable for children of all ages.

TV Y7 Material suitable for children seven and older.

TV G Material suitable for all audiences.

TV PG Parental guidance is suggested.

TV 14 Material may be inapproriate for children under fourteen.

TV MA Programs designed to be viewed by mature audiences and that may be unsuitable for children under seventeen.

In addition to the above age-based ratings symbols, programs may also carry the following designations to forewarn of potentially objectionable content: "V" for violence, "S" for sexual situations, "L" for coarse language, "D" for sexually suggesetive dialogue, and "FV" for fantasy violence on children's programs.

Source: CQ Researcher, August 15, 1997.

And there aren't many such executives left. Only NBC and Black Entertainment Television (BET) are still refusing to provide content ratings. Most in the industry believe, as the president of ABC has said, that ratings are not going to change the way they do business. Advertisers will continue to support quality shows, and adult programming will continue to be provided to adult audiences. If ratings and blocking mean a broadcaster or cable network loses young viewers for whom the programming is not intended, where is the harm?

Not a Panacea

This is not a panacea, nor is it a substitute for teaching children the difference between right and wrong. But neither is it the government telling the industry what to put on the air. Any broadcaster can continue to provide adult programming. The rights of adults to see programming that is violent or sexual are preserved, while the rights of parents to shield their 5-year-olds from that same material also are protected.

As technology evolves, society will continually need to find ways to balance both the good and the evil that technology facilitates. Television is not exempt. All America benefits from free over-the-air television. It is universally available—a great benefit—but also pervasive. By the time the average American child leaves elementary school, he or she has witnessed 8,000 murders and 100,000 acts of televised violence. Ratings and the V-chip help busy parents restore a measure of control over this mayhem without intruding on the rights of producers.

The First Amendment was not compromised by the "on-off" button. I am confident it will survive this simple upgrade of the "on-off" button for today's world of 100-channel TVs, single parents and working couples.

PERIODICAL BIBLIOGRAPHY

The following articles have been selected to supplement the diverse views presented in this chapter. Addresses are provided for periodicals not indexed in the *Readers' Guide to Periodical Literature*, the *Alternative Press Index*, the *Social Sciences Index*, or the *Index to Legal Periodicals and Books*.

Dan Andriacco	"V-Chips Short-Circuit Parental Responsibility," *U.S. Catholic*, June 1996.
David Bender	"Censor Vision," *George*, March 1997. Available from 30 Montgomery St., Jersey City, NJ 07032.
Sidney Callahan	"What We See, We Do," *Commonweal*, January 12, 1996.
Mona Charen	"TV Ratings Don't Solve Problem," *Conservative Chronicle*, December 25, 1996. Available from PO Box 29, Hampton, IA 50441.
George Dessart	"Reflections on the V-Chip," *Television Quarterly*, vol. 28, no. 3, 1996.
Barbara Dority and John Perry Barlow	"Ratings and the V-Chip," *Humanist*, May/June 1996.
Laurie J. Flynn	"V-Chip and Ratings Are Close to Giving Parents New Power," *New York Times*, April 2, 1998.
Nick Gillespie	"Information Rage: Rating the TV Raters," *Reason*, March 1997.
Peter A. Lund	"New TV Ratings Are Parent-Friendly," *New York Times*, December 18, 1996.
Dyan Machan	"Mr. Valenti Goes to Washington," *Forbes*, December 1, 1997.
Julian Petley	"It May Be Hi-Tech, It Ain't Sense," *Index on Censorship*, March 1996.
Elizabeth A. Rathbun	"Parents Don't Understand, Study Concludes," *Broadcasting and Cable*, June 9, 1997. Available from 1705 DeSales St. NW, Washington, DC 20036.
Carl Rowan	"The Fraudulent War over TV Sex and Violence," *Liberal Opinion*, March 11, 1996. Available from PO Box 880, Vinton, IA 52349-0880.
Daniel T. Wackerman	"God Forbid That Anything Remotely Lewd or Gratuitously Violent Should Appear on the Old Zenith," *America*, March 2, 1996.
Richard Zoglin	"Rating Wars," *Time*, December 23, 1996.

CHAPTER 3

How Should Society Respond to Media Violence?

CHAPTER PREFACE

How to ensure the well-being of America's children has been a primary focus of public discussion concerning violent television shows, motion pictures, video games, and other forms of violence in the media. Educators and organizations such as the Minnesota Medical Association have published and distributed tips for parents concerned about media violence. Suggestions range from setting strict rules limiting children's exposure to media violence to watching television with one's children and talking with them about what they are viewing. Some families have resorted to doing without television or movies altogether.

While most Americans would agree that parents bear the primary responsibility for protecting their children from media violence, controversy remains over whether other members of society should also be held accountable. Some commentators argue that parents are solely responsible for their children's well-being. For example, Dick Wolf, a television producer whose shows include the police drama *Law and Order*, stated in a 1994 panel discussion on television violence that he did not allow his own children, then ages five and eight, to watch the shows he produced. A strong opponent of outside regulation of the media, he maintains that "parents are supposed to monitor what their children are doing."

However, others contend that parents by themselves cannot be expected to protect their children from media violence all the time. Many agree with syndicated columnist Ellen Goodman's observation that the "call for parental responsibility is increasing in direct proportion to the irresponsibility of the marketplace." Goodman and others question whether parents should be expected "to screen virtually every aspect of their children's lives." They maintain that other elements of society, especially the media industry itself, should hold at least some responsibility for ensuring that media violence does not harm America's children.

Most people agree that media violence is an issue that cannot be ignored, regardless of whether monitoring children's exposure is a problem for individual families or society as a whole. The viewpoints in the following chapter examine various ways in which families, the entertainment industry, schools, and other social institutions can act both to reduce the amount of media violence that children view and to mitigate its allegedly harmful effects.

"Fortunately, most media violence can
be turned off."

PARENTS SHOULD RESTRICT THEIR CHILDREN'S EXPOSURE TO MEDIA VIOLENCE

National Crime Prevention Council

Parents can and should prevent their children from being exposed to media violence, according to the following viewpoint by the National Crime Prevention Council (NCPC). The violence found in television shows, computer and video games, radio broadcasts, and other media poses a threat to young people, the NCPC maintains. It urges that parents closely examine what their children are watching and restrict their exposure to violent programming. The organization also provides suggestions on how parents can influence their children's viewing habits and encourage alternative activities to watching television and movies. The NCPC is a private, nonprofit association that provides schools and the public with educational resources on crime prevention.

As you read, consider the following questions:

1. What questions should parents ask about the television shows and movies they watch, according to the NCPC?
2. According to the NCPC, what is the most important influence on children's viewing habits?
3. What actions does the NCPC recommend that parents take concerning media violence?

Reprinted from the National Crime Prevention Council, "Turning Off Media Violence," at www.ncpc.org/1safe6dc.htm, cited February 4, 1998, by permission.

For too many people, violence is an ordinary way to be entertained, settle arguments, or blow off steam.

Violence results when many different forces come together, and we know that exposure to violence in the media can be one of those forces. American children spend more time each week watching television than in any other activity except sleeping. But violence isn't limited to TV—it can be found in music, video games, newspapers, comic books, radio broadcasts, magazines, movies, and the real world.

Exposing children to violence can make them less sensitive to the pain and suffering of others, more fearful of the world around them, and more willing to act aggressively. Fortunately, most media violence can be turned off.

LOOK AT WHAT YOU ARE WATCHING

Take a hard look at what you and your family watch on TV—action movies, talk shows, sitcoms, cop shows, and even news programs. Ask the same questions about movies, video tapes, comics, and computer and video games.

- What values are they teaching? Are the characters racist, sexist, or stereotypical?
- Do they make violence appear exciting or humorous or macho?
- Do they solve real-life problems without violence?
- Do the programs show how the victims of violence, their families, and their friends suffer?
- Do the programs teach skills or convey unique, valuable, interesting information?

TECHNOLOGY CAN HELP

Hi-tech tools can help parents monitor what their children are watching. The newest device being developed is the V-chip, which allows the TV to be programmed to block shows that are rated high in violence, sex, or other material not suited for young viewers. Many cable companies already offer parents the option of "locking out" channels they don't want their children to see. This is done through scrambling channels (parents can access with a key), blocking out specific cable channels on request, or using programmable remote controls which can be overridden with a personal identification number. Similar technology exists to filter Internet material.

However, nothing can take the place of parents when it comes to influencing children's habits.

USE TV'S INCREDIBLE POTENTIAL TO EDUCATE

- Ask teachers what they will be covering in the upcoming school year. Look for TV specials and videos on the topics. Talk to teachers or school librarians about videos that enrich your child's studies in school.
- Use everyday viewing to tie into children's school lessons. Ask them questions as they watch TV. Does today's news have something in common with what's being studied in history class? How is a television program different than a book on the same subject? How do television producers get their message across compared to writers and artists?
- Use TV to encourage your children to read. Sometimes a child will get excited about something they viewed on TV. Follow up that excitement by taking them to the library to check out books on the same subject.
- If your child has a particular interest or hobby, tape shows that relate to it. A budding ballerina may enjoy watching a professional dance group perform or a child who collects and plays with dinosaurs may enjoy a movie on how dinosaurs became extinct.

TAKE ACTION

- Turn off violent television, radio, and movies that you think send dangerous messages to children about violence and its

Reprinted by permission of Mike Luckovich and Creators Syndicate.

victims. Tell radio and television stations and movie theaters about your decision through calls and letters. Also use calls and letters to thank the media when they show programming that portrays positive, nonviolent ways of solving problems. Encourage the media to provide more family-related programming and show positive actions by people to improve the community.

- Contact your local school to see if it has a mediation or conflict resolution program. If not, help start one. You can get information, training, and materials from colleges, community or neighborhood dispute resolution centers, or national organizations that focus on dispute resolution.
- Make one night a month a family night. Why not go to dinner, go for a walk, take in a nonviolent movie, play board or card games? Play volleyball, ping pong, or a game of catch, go to the library, read aloud, or go through old family photos and slides? Ask everyone in the family for suggestions.
- Don't buy products whose advertisements glorify physical or verbal violence. Write the manufacturer to express your concern. Check product packages or call your local library for addresses.
- Work with a local church, business, or civic group to sponsor a violent toy turn-in drive. Ask a local business to donate gift certificates for a nonviolent toy, a book, or sports equipment.

"Parents need to help their children become consumers of media, making thoughtful ... choices about programs that are of real interest to them."

PARENTS SHOULD GUIDE THEIR CHILDREN'S TELEVISION VIEWING

Madeline Levine

Psychologist Madeline Levine is the author of *Viewing Violence: How Media Violence Affects Your Child's and Adolescent's Development*, from which the following viewpoint is taken. Levine provides suggestions on how parents can minimize the harmful effects of media violence on their children. Parents should watch television with their children to learn about what they are watching, comment and interact with their children while watching programs together, and teach them that television viewing should be a directed and purposeful activity, Levine recommends. Despite the number of violent shows, she claims, there are also many positive and worthwhile television programs that parents can encourage their children to watch.

As you read, consider the following questions:

1. What social values do most people agree are important, according to Levine?
2. How does watching TV with children help them learn to behave better, according to the author?
3. Why is it important for parents to plan together with their children what television programs they will watch, in Levine's opinion?

It is relatively easy to identify a problem as major as media violence and its effects on youth. It is even reasonably easy to describe such a problem; evaluate existing research, draw from personal and professional experience, and consult the experts. But it is extraordinarily difficult to come up with suggestions and solutions that have any "teeth" in them. . . .

I would like to offer suggestions for changes that parents can make. This is because, in the final analysis, it is parents, not media executives, not Madison Avenue, and not corporate America, who are most concerned with the welfare of their children. The responsibility of raising, protecting, and educating children has always been the family's. Obviously, the family has never functioned alone but is set within a larger context of both a particular social group and society at large. . . .

WHAT PARENTS CAN DO

It would be wonderful if parents could all march to Hollywood and demand better programming for their children. Galvanizing the entertainment industry would seem to be the most efficient way of making sweeping changes in the nature of children's television. However, it seems unlikely that we will be seeing "television violence can be hazardous to your health" warnings on our screens any time in the near future.

How can we encourage programming that meets the developmental needs of children and is in accordance with most parents' values? Surveys show that in spite of the diversity of opinion in this country, there is actually a great deal of consensus on what "good values" are. Loyalty, responsibility, family, integrity, and courage are all high on the list of values that parents say they want to see in their children. There are few who would quibble with these values. In 1992, top leaders of youth and education groups, under the guidance of the Josephson Institute, met to formulate a character education program. They named six values that they believe define good character. Called the "Six Pillars of Character," they are trustworthiness, respect, responsibility, fairness, caring, and citizenship. So it seems that parents, educators, youth leaders, and ethics scholars all pretty much agree on the character traits that produce "good" human beings and therefore a more vital and resilient society. How are we failing to communicate those values to our children? And how can we use the media to reinforce those values we consider important rather than supplant them with confusing and often antisocial messages?

The following list of suggestions, all supported by research as well as by common sense, is intended as a guide for parents who would like to lessen the negative effects and encourage the positive effects of media for their children.

WATCH TELEVISION WITH YOUR CHILDREN

Research studies have repeatedly shown that parents are not particularly interested in what their children watch. The majority of parents do not monitor their children's television viewing. The most frequent interventions parents make with regard to television are rules about how late their children can stay up and watch. It is unrealistic to expect parents to watch everything their children watch. However, in order to take a stand about television viewing or movies, we have to see enough to have a leg to stand on. I suggest that parents spend a week or two getting an idea of what their children are watching. Are your children channel surfing out of boredom? Is their viewing more selective, and what kinds of selections are they making? A steady diet of situation comedies is different from a steady diet of adventure and action shows. And even within these genres there are substantial differences. *Full House* is a far cry from *Married . . . with Children*. Situation comedies are, by far, the most frequently watched programs for children of all ages. Children need help discriminating between humor that entertains and teaches and humor that insults and humiliates.

What children watch depends on many factors, including age, gender, interest, and what's available. Unlike almost all other forms of entertainment, television viewing tends to be a nonselective ritual. Kids with spare time turn it on not to view a particular program but to kill time. This is a particularly poor use of television because it encourages indiscriminate viewing.

Once parents are familiar with what their children are watching, at what times, and under what circumstances (boredom? relaxation? background noise?) they can develop a plan to help their children avoid the worst of what TV offers and enjoy the best.

ADVANTAGES OF WATCHING TV TOGETHER

Aside from arming ourselves with information about what our kids see, watching with our children serves their development in a number of well-documented ways.

Watching with children increases comprehension. Several researchers studied children over a two-year period and found that when parents watch with their children, *and actively discuss and explain* what they're viewing, the youngsters' understanding of television content improves. Parental involvement also improves children's judgments about reality and fantasy, increases prosocial behavior, and lessens the desire to watch television altogether. These findings were particularly compelling for boys. This may be because girls' verbal abilities are evident earlier, and they may need less explanation in order to understand the programs they watch.

Simply sitting in the same room with a child while he or she watches television is not likely to be beneficial. Parents need to comment, explain, and interpret in an active process of interaction with their children. The media, television in particular, pour into our homes and into the minds of our children. Without parents helping children sort out and understand the many messages that are delivered, children are vulnerable to misunderstanding much of what they see.

DRAWING DISTINCTIONS BETWEEN TELEVISION SHOWS

A parent, or someone acting as a parent, doesn't have to be mechanistic. Parents . . . can draw distinctions guided by love, values, and sense. They can appreciate that good TV programs sometimes include violence that should not be harmful to children if part of a balanced media diet. Handled realistically and not glamorized, violence can have a place in serious drama-like *Homicide: Life on the Streets*. More often, though, guns and fists are an easy way for writers to move the story along, stimulate the viewer, and establish the heroes as macho, á la *Power Rangers*.

Perhaps parents should block out such programs. But first they should watch a few episodes with their children and explain, in a way appropriate to each child's age, why this devaluing of life is wrong and not welcome in their family room. Yes, parents should watch television with their children. There probably should be only one TV in the home and certainly not one in each child's room to magnify the fragmentation already an unwelcome part of family life. Sometimes at the end of a program parents should turn off the set and discuss what they've all seen. (Why did the hero resort to violence? What were the other options? What would Jesus have done?)

Dan Andriacco, *U.S. Catholic*, June 1996.

Watching with children decreases stereotypical thinking. The power of television to provide children with stereotypes is greatest when children have few other sources of information. Stereotypes, like aggression, are learned early and are difficult to correct. When my nine-year-old son saw the movie *Dances with Wolves*, he was fascinated by hearing the language of the Sioux. "I never really thought about it. I guess I thought they just spoke English," he said. The message most of us grew up with was that cowboys are good guys and Indians are bad guys. Recently there have been some efforts to correct these stereotypes, often equally unrealistic in their portrayal of Native American culture. Kevin Costner's movie was the first time that many children in this country had any exposure to a sympathetic but unsentimental view of Native American life. Parents watching this movie with their children were given a tremendous opportunity to talk about the ways in which the media promote ideas about groups of people and how often these ideas are inaccurate. Movies like this can be a wonderful jumping-off place for discussions, for trips to a museum, and especially for further reading on the subject.

PROSOCIAL MESSAGES

Watching with children increases prosocial behavior. A number of studies have shown that watching television programs with prosocial messages increases cooperation, sensitivity, and caring among children. *Mister Rogers' Neighborhood* is a program that has been scrupulously studied by social scientists, who find that as little as two weeks of watching this program helps preschoolers to be more cooperative, nurturing, and better able to express their feelings. It also helps children to "follow the rules," stick with a task, and tolerate frustration. *Barney and Friends,* written by a team of early childhood education specialists, has been shown to enhance not only cognitive development but emotional and social development as well. With the show's attention to safety issues, Barney has taught children as young as two to warn family members about house fires. Other studies have shown that even older children and adolescents are positively influenced by prosocial portrayals.

Researchers have found that while children tend to learn aggression simply by watching it, they learn prosocial behavior far more effectively when it is combined with additional reinforcements such as role-playing and discussion. While rivers of ink have been written on the effects of media violence on children, there has been barely a trickle of interest in the effects of prosocial television. This is unfortunate because *prosocial portrayals have a potentially larger effect on children than antisocial portrayals.* Parents need to choose more prosocial programming and encourage their children to adopt the prosocial behaviors they see. Exposing children to prosocial programs and helping them interpret what they see is one way to diminish the enduring power of early aggressive television messages. In addition, prosocial messages nurture a sense of optimism, which is critical for children's healthy psychological development. . . .

A TELEVISION DIET

The American Academy of Pediatrics recommends that children's viewing be restricted to two hours per day or less. Many other organizations and researchers working on this issue have come to the same conclusion. . . .

One way to limit the amount of television that children watch is to put them on a television diet, modeled after a food diet. The analogy allows us to recognize that it is more complex than simply turning off the bad stuff and only watching good stuff. Diets make us aware that we have different kinds of needs. Mostly we eat for nutrition, but sometimes we eat for pleasure and sometimes we eat for comfort.

Similarly, our children ought to be using television primarily to educate and inform (this doesn't mean only "educational TV," with its connotation of one too many animal specials) by watching programs that stimulate their thinking. There are a host of amusing, informative programs for kids to watch, and parents need to become familiar with them. . . .

TEACH CHILDREN TO WATCH WITH A PURPOSE

Television is a vehicle, a means to an end; it is not a way of life. Many children sit for hours at a time, mindlessly channel surfing their way through life, as opposed to living it. Children need to be taught that the television, just like every other appliance in the house, has a specific function. We do not leave the hair dryer on once our hair is dry, or the toaster on once the toast has popped up. We recognize the specific uses of these appliances and know when to shut them off. Our children need to be similarly educated about television.

One way to begin teaching this is to sit with our children and go over the programs they are interested in seeing. Look at *TV Guide* or your local television listings and make decisions about what your children's television week will look like. Some parents are quite successful at holding their children to a number of choices that they agree on. Others find that accommodations and changes can be made over the course of the week. Either way, the exercise of sitting down together and making decisions about what children will watch teaches a very valuable lesson. It teaches children that television viewing is a directed activity. Allowing even young children to participate in this exercise makes it clear from the beginning of their relationship with television that television is not a device that we passively allow to fill up dead space; rather, it is a source of entertainment and education that we actively pursue. Parents need to help their children become consumers of media, making thoughtful and economical choices about programs that are of real interest to them. Often that means thinking about our own choices as well.

> "More insidious than violence and twisted values is the way TV separates us from intimacy and interaction."

FAMILIES SHOULD ATTEMPT TO LIVE WITHOUT TELEVISION

Chiori Santiago

Some individuals and organizations have reacted to the problem of television violence by encouraging families to quit watching television altogether. A Washington, D.C.–based organization called TV-Free America, for example, sponsors an annual National TV-Turn-Off Week, during which parents and children in participating schools and communities are urged to abstain from watching television and to pursue alternative activities. In the following viewpoint, Chiori Santiago expresses her support for this idea even as she admits that such a step would be difficult for her. She cites concerns about the negative effects that television and its constant references to violence have on children. Breaking the TV-viewing habit, she contends, can help families grow closer. Santiago is a writer who contributes regularly to the "Family Matters" column of *Diablo*, a monthly magazine that covers the East Bay area of San Francisco, California.

As you read, consider the following questions:

1. What does Santiago find appealing about television?
2. What two incidents caused the author to consider a break from television?
3. What lessons about conflict resolution does television teach, according to the author?

Reprinted from Chiori Santiago, "Family Matters," *Diablo*, April 1997, by permission of the author.

I f you're the parent of a child in Contra Costa's public schools, you'll soon be receiving an important notice reminding you that April 21–28, 1997, is TV Turn-Off Week. Organized by concerned Orinda, California, mom and political activist Ellen Schwartz, the event is a plea for families to take a vacation from the mayhem and merchandising of television for seven days. It's an important effort, and I urge you to take part.

I hope I will be doing the same, but I'm doubting my stamina.

AN ADDICT'S ADMISSION

I love television. Always have. As I write this, the television is on in the next room, its steady drone of canned laughter and peppy theme music creating a friendly ambience in the empty house, its intermittent flicker as soothing as candlelight. I'm sure that television's resemblance to the hearth fulfills some deep and primitive yearning in the human soul. Take a walk through the neighborhood at night and you sense its ever presence; behind venetian blinds and picture windows the blue glow beckons, asking us to sit hypnotized by dancing light and listen to the lull of the griot's tales—even if they're corrupted by commercials for athletic shoes and panty liners.

I admit, I'm an addict. To get me through TV Turn-Off Week I'll need one of those electronic monitors they give to petty criminals. It'll sound an alarm when I rise and sneak through the sleeping house to catch Conan O'Brien's monologue or the revelatory climax of *All About Eve*. "Just a little fix, please," I can hear myself say. I will do my best to maintain a moral steadfastness as long my kids are awake. I will brightly unplug the set and suggest a game of Scrabble. The minute they're tucked in, though, I'm afraid I'll revert like a skid row junkie in a sea of denial for one little nip at my bottle of electronic comfort.

Hypocrites like me have a bagful of justifications. Look at all that's wonderful about television, I say. By what other means can you, in a single evening, take a train ride across Russia or learn about a distant galaxy far, far away? Television can pique the imagination, it's informative, and it's overrated as a fount of evil. Television has never compelled me to corporate consumerism (the only product label I look for is the one that says "50% Off") or to copycat crime. I've seen my sister-in-law do all her high school homework while watching TV, listening to a Walkman and talking on the telephone—simultaneously—and she got straight As.

Television isn't so much bad as it is mindless. What bothers me is not the level of distasteful content, but the lack of content.

Mainstream programming features three themes: people or animals killing each other, people winning things and people making fools of themselves. I'm amazed that with sixty-four cable channels, there's nothing worth watching on Saturday night. Therefore, I'm pretty ambivalent about the medium; I think TV Turn-Off Week is a great idea—for someone else. But recently, two incidents made me think that Ellen Schwartz has a point.

Two Disturbing Incidents

I was in the backyard with my six-year-old son a few weekends ago when we heard someone coughing loudly in another yard. It was an intrusive, rabid kind of cough, to be sure, but nothing out of the ordinary, I thought. My son had a different theory.

"I think someone's being murdered," he said.

That upset me. What he said was disturbing enough, but I was really bothered by the way he said it, with an air of nonchalance, as if the sound of someone being murdered two yards over was a sound you'd expect to hear on a quiet Sunday.

Why not? Murder, as relayed by television, has been a constant part of my son's environment. He hears about it every night on the six o'clock news, in advertisements for the movie of the week. Cartoon characters spend whole half hours trying to wipe out each other. The horror of death dissolves in the surreal life of television programming. . . . Try as we do to monitor his viewing, restricting him to the Disney channel and Nickelodeon, the violent world intrudes. Murder is just another fact of life for him, no more remarkable than a school lunch.

The other incident happened when I called the kid for dinner and he was so absorbed in the tube that he didn't respond. Now, you can talk about how TV rots your brain and leads to smoking, short attention span and obesity, and I'll say, "Pshaw." But let it lead to a kid not listening to his mother and, believe me, TV is in big trouble.

So, I went to see Ellen Schwartz. She runs a nonprofit organization called Healing Our Nation from Violence out of an office in Walnut Creek, California, that barely holds a very large desk and an even more expansive personality. Schwartz is the kind of person who could make you swallow cod liver oil and love it—not because it's good for you, but because her sheer enthusiasm sweeps you up in the zeal of her crusade.

How Children Respond to TV Violence

Schwartz . . . is no temperance fanatic. She, too, grew up in the age of television and loved it as much as I do. She remembers getting up early on beautiful summer days to pour a bowl of cereal and hunker down to watch cartoons. "But there's such an important difference between the TV we watched and the TV our kids watch," she says. "We saw the consequences of violence. Now there are no consequences. We don't see the shattered lives and disabilities. Nowadays, comedy is put-downs followed by a laugh track. Fifty-two percent of the nightly news is devoted to mayhem: rape, robbery, war. Children don't see compassion. That's when we have anger and alienation."

TAKE A STEP AGAINST TELEVISION VIOLENCE

Our children are inundated. By the time they've graduated from high school, they've seen 200,000 acts of violence on TV alone, including 30,000 murders.

Just what is this doing to the hearts and minds of our children?

Sure, most kids don't grow up to be assault weapon murderers, but the effects are real, in how they relate and in how they solve problems. . . .

This problem is large, but it need not be overwhelming. Whether you choose to take a small step or a large one, each action is important.

Examine your own TV viewing habits and your children's, and take the leap to participate in the National TV Turn-Off Week. . . .

Television is only one facet contributing to the violence in our lives. But in its pervasiveness, it is something we cannot ignore. Our children are too precious.

Ellen Schwartz, *San Francisco Examiner*, April 24, 1996.

Kids' models of conflict resolution come from these shows, according to Schwartz. A script in which people are shown discussing their feelings and working out problems won't hold our attention long enough to sell a jar of peanut butter, so television captures attention with a steady rhythm of shootings, seductions or pratfalls. "When this is the predominant model, you're not getting realistic conflict resolution," she says. Hence, an increase in violence, disrespect, apathy and a fixation on instant gratification that everyone from the American Medical Association to the Congress of National Black Churches to the National Association of Elementary School Principals says is leading to a culture in which caring and interaction are outmoded concepts.

That realization led Schwartz to create an ad hoc TV turn-off effort in 1987. "When my son was nine we had such battles over what he could and couldn't watch," she explains. "During one of these battles my husband said, 'Fine, let's just get the TV out of the house.' We'd sit on the deck and watch the stars. We dusted off the bikes, and instead of sitting and eating ice cream in front of the tube, we rode into town and bought cones. We spoke to each other!"

The TV's back, and Schwartz's husband and son continue to indulge in routine doses of sports programs and cheesy sitcoms. On the other hand, her daughter, now nine, grew up without television's constant presence and isn't dependent on it for entertainment. Reason enough, Schwartz thinks, to put TV in its place and turn attention to alternative entertainment that can bring us together as families.

More insidious than violence and twisted values is the way TV separates us from intimacy and interaction. I think of all the times I've used television to buy a little time away from my kids. I've used it, essentially, to ignore them. Should I be surprised when my son uses it to ignore me?

THE PERFECT ADDICTION

TV is the perfect addiction. There we sit, slack-jawed, pupils dilated, in a suburban version of an opium den, avoiding problems and conversation. "It controls the room," Schwartz says. "No one gets up from the TV refreshed and renewed. Instead, they're disgruntled. They're lethargic. It is hypnotic. Kids will lie to be able to watch TV. And most of all, it's not an addiction you have to admit, because we all have it.

"Television robs us of life. Why are we spending so many hours watching other people's lives instead of exploring the gifts of the people we care about?"

TV Turn-Off Week is not meant as punishment. The information packet schoolchildren will bring home contains lists of alternative things to do (my favorites: "clean up your room" and "think"), good discussion questions for teachers and convincing arguments for people like me, pointing out that it isn't the black box that's criminal—it's the way we let it control us.

"TV Turn-Off Week gives us a break," says Schwartz. "We're all such mysteries; the little hurts and confusions and frustrations often come out when we talk to each other. We need enough quiet time to figure out our passions. Turning off the TV is a promise to be there for your kids. They want time with us more than anything."

Will I be able to live one week without Helen Mirren and Dennis Richmond? I'm not sure. I will make a pledge, though. I promise to listen to my son pick his way through *The Foot Book* for the seventeenth time, to pay attention when my husband explains the fine points of a 1-3-1 zone trap in basketball, and to hear the murmurings of the house at night, the little creakings and shiftings that, in the absence of TV, whisper a reminder that this place is a home.

"[Media violence] is a major public health concern requiring that appropriate steps be taken now."

MEDIA VIOLENCE SHOULD BE TREATED AS A PUBLIC HEALTH PROBLEM

American Medical Association

The American Medical Association (AMA) is the largest professional association of medical doctors in the United States. In the following viewpoint, taken from a 1995 position statement given before a U.S. Senate committee, the AMA asserts that media violence is a significant problem that contributes to the prevalence of violence in America. Arguing that violence should be treated as a public health issue as well as a criminal justice concern, the AMA calls for educational campaigns designed to increase public awareness about the dangers of media violence, much as similar programs have warned against drunk driving and tobacco use. The organization also contends that media and advertising companies should reduce the amount of violence found in television and other forms of media.

As you read, consider the following questions:

1. How does the AMA define "virtual violence"?
2. What are some of the lasting psychological and physiological effects of repeated exposures to media violence, according to the AMA?
3. What legislative reforms does the AMA endorse?

Reprinted from the American Medical Association's statement in *Television Violence*, a hearing before the U.S. Senate Committee on Commerce, Science, and Transportation, July 12, 1995.

The American Medical Association (AMA) appreciates the opportunity to submit this statement to the Senate Commerce Committee for the record on the important issue of "violence in the media." We have termed this issue "Virtual Violence," or violence that appears in various forms of media entertainment such as television, music, film, video, computer and cyberspace. This type of violence refers to violence that is not directly experienced, but which may create a lasting psycho-social effect on individual viewers. . . .

VIRTUAL VIOLENCE

The sad fact is that, over the course of time, violence has been imperceptively woven into the fabric of our nation and permeates every aspect of our daily lives, including many of our sources of entertainment. The general public intuitively understands this; in a national poll, 79% of Americans indicated that they believed that violence in the media directly contributes to the problem of actual violence in our society. The AMA believes that violence, including "virtual violence," has become a major medical and public health epidemic.

Clearly, American society has had enough of violence. The AMA shares this frustration. In a national poll, Americans listed crime as the number one problem facing society. Indeed, from the physician's point of view, we are the ones asked to mend the broken bones and stitch the lacerations only to have many of these victims return shortly thereafter to the emergency room or morgue. The statistics on violence are staggering. As a nation, the United States ranks first among all developed countries in the world in homicides. In 1991 there were more than 5.8 million violent crimes, including 21,505 homicides. Among individuals 15 to 24 years old, homicide is the second leading cause of death, and for African-American youth it is number one. Over 2 million people in this country each year suffer from violent nonfatal injuries.

There are many factors that help to determine violent behavior. In general, studies have shown that drugs and alcohol, guns, poverty, racism, family and community environment all may play a part. The U.S. Surgeon General, the National Institutes of Mental Health, the National Academy of Science, the Centers for Disease Control and Prevention, and the Society of Adolescent Medicine have all conducted independent scientific research documenting the relationship between mass media and violent behavior. In addition, organizations such as the Centers for Disease Control and Prevention, the American Psychiatric Association and the American Psychological Association have also concluded that the mass media violence is an integral and detrimental part of our nation's culture of violence.

Clinically speaking, it has been shown that the normal physiological signs of emotional and physical reactions disappear over time with the continuous, chronic and habitual exposure to media violence. In general, the so-called "flight-fight" response is triggered when an individual views an act of violence, whether they are standing on the street corner or at home watching television. This involuntary response is triggered by stimuli which individuals reflexively experience, including an immediate increase and acceleration of the heart beat, constriction of the arteries raising the blood pressure, slowing of the digestive tract, relaxation of the bladder, dilation of the airways and pupils, increased sweat gland secretion and hair standing on end. After enough and repeated exposure to violent acts, the viewer, whether a child or an adult, experiences a desensitization to the emotional reactions that aggression and violence normally produce.

It is a shocking fact that by the time children leave elementary school, they have seen 8,000 killings and 100,000 other violent acts portrayed on television, according to the Center for Media and Public Affairs. The same source reports that by the age of 18, the typical American child will have witnessed 40,000 killings and 200,000 acts of violence on television. It is a well accepted principle that children learn behavior by example. The pairing of the learning by example with the decreased physiologic response is what makes this exposure of such great concern. . . . Of course, the AMA does not maintain that "virtual violence" is the only cause of violence in society. We do maintain, however, that such violence is a highly intense and pervasive factor, and may particularly influence the young and susceptible. . . .

WHAT CAN BE DONE

The AMA believes that because violence is a public health threat, similar techniques used to discourage the use of tobacco and drunk driving must be employed and will require a multi-year strategy to be successful. As a part of this strategy, we maintain that careful consideration must be given to the content of television programs, movies, or music. For example, in 1993, the AMA supported efforts by network broadcasters in adopting an "Advance Parental Advisory" prior to airing programs that are unfit for children in which each network determines the appropriate use of the advisory. As we said at the time, we view the

ABC-CBS-NBC-Fox agreement as a start toward helping parents become involved in making more informed decisions for their children, but merely a start. If parents are not there when the advisory appears, the children will be making the choice rather than the parents. In addition, the advisory does little or next to nothing to reduce violent programming and might not extend to all such programming, like cartoons, which mesmerize children on a daily basis.

MEDIA VIOLENCE AND THE PUBLIC HEALTH PERSPECTIVE

We can't know how much societal violence is actually caused by media violence. Yet our inability to pinpoint cause and effect so precisely has not stood in the way of discussing and promoting policies to curtail cigarette smoking and drunk driving; it is not clear, therefore, why it should block policy debates about TV violence. . . .

In the past few years, scholars, community advocates, health care professionals, and public officials have increasingly come to view the problems of violence from a public health perspective, in addition to legal and other perspectives. The public health perspective, long familiar with respect to heart disease, cancer, motor vehicle injuries, and other major causes of death and disability, allows a wide-ranging and integrated exploration of the incidence of different forms of violence, of possible risk factors, and of approaches to risk reduction and prevention.

Sissela Bok, *American Prospect*, Spring 1994.

The AMA has also been supportive of "TV Turn-Off Week," which was designed to replace television viewing with more healthy, family-oriented activities. Although this event does not deal specifically with the problem of media violence, TV Turn-Off Week does limit exposure to television violence.

The AMA and other anti-violence organizations co-sponsored "Voices Against Violence," which was begun in 1994 by the cable television programmers. It is a program designed to reduce and deglamorize media violence. As part of the initiative, nearly 50 cable networks participated in "Voices Against Violence Week" in early 1995, which devoted a week of programming to the examination of societal violence.

The AMA has publicly stated that it supports a proposal to install in televisions computer chips ("Violence" or "V" Chips) that can screen out violent programming. Use of the "V" Chip would be optional. The AMA has also called upon the Federal

Communications Commission (FCC) to consider establishing a violence rating system for television and cable programming or other ways to limit viewership of violent programming. We would also support the establishment of guidelines for broadcasters to follow in programming during prime time and children's viewing hours. We would suggest that compliance with these guidelines be tied to license renewal or revocation, with the potential levying of monetary fines against cable and TV broadcasters who fail to comply with the guidelines. Furthermore, we call upon TV advertisers to act in a responsible manner and ask that they refrain from expending advertising monies for violent television programs, thereby encouraging the reduction in the amount of violence on television. . . .

A TOP PRIORITY

The AMA has actively made combating violence one of our top priorities. The AMA maintains that "virtual violence" is a major public health concern requiring that appropriate steps be taken now. Analysis of the current research supports the conclusion that there is a positive association between televised violence exposure and aggressive behavior across a wide range of ages and measures of aggressive behavior. The research also shows that exposure to violent programming increases aggressive behavior and is associated with lower levels of socially acceptable behavior. We believe that a balance must be struck between individual rights of expression and social responsibility. We also maintain that this balance can only be achieved if Americans are provided with the tools needed to allow them to distinguish between those forms of entertainment that may be suitable to their own tastes, and which they may deem appropriate for their families. As Dr. Robert McAffee, AMA President, has said about combating violence, "Alone we can do nothing. Together we can do anything."

| "Self-regulation is common sense, not censorship."

THE MEDIA INDUSTRY SHOULD EXERCISE SELF-RESTRAINT

Joseph Lieberman

The issue of media violence, Joseph Lieberman argues in the following viewpoint, is part of a more general concern: The nation's television, motion picture, and music recording industries are producing products that are disgusting and disturbing to most Americans. Many parents, he maintains, feel helpless trying to instill values in their children in the face of what they view as an onslaught of violence, sex, and crude language from the media. He urges the media industry to take the initiative in addressing the concerns of parents by creating a self-regulatory system that would limit media depictions of violence and other offensive materials. Lieberman is a Democratic senator representing Connecticut.

As you read, consider the following questions:

1. What does the "V" in V-chip stand for, according to the author?
2. What suggestions does Lieberman make to the TV industry about its programming practices?
3. What opinion does Lieberman express about the prospect of government censorship of the media?

Reprinted from Joseph Lieberman, "Why Parents Hate TV," *Policy Review*, May/June 1996, by permission of *Policy Review*.

Over the past few months of 1995 and 1996, the V-chip [a device that can selectively block television program reception] has quickly become the most celebrated piece of computer circuitry in America. In swift succession, President Bill Clinton championed this little byte of technology in his State of the Union address in January 1996, Congress passed legislation mandating its use, and the major networks grumbled loudly about challenging the law in court. The drama finally culminated in February 1996 at a summit at the White House, where the TV industry's chieftains grudgingly accepted the president's challenge to do more for America's parents and create a ratings system compatible with the V-chip.

The story of the V-chip unfolded so fast, and its potential impact is so great, that the media has spent most of its time struggling to answer a host of basic questions: How does this signal-blocking technology work? When will it be available? How much will it cost? Will it live up to its billing? Some are still not even sure what the "V" actually stands for. (It originally stood for "violence," but it seems everyone has their own interpretation. I hope it comes to mean "values.")

As a Senate cosponsor of the V-chip bill along with Democrat Kent Conrad, I know these details matter, but I also believe the media's focus on them has obscured a larger point. Far more important than what the "V" stands for is what the coming of the V-chip tells us about the public's plummeting regard for the product that television delivers to our homes. Although this invention may merely be an irritant to those in the television business, to millions of Americans the V-chip is a surrogate for their anger at the entertainment industry for degrading our culture and our society.

ANGER AT THE MEDIA

That anger is clearly reflected in any number of public opinion polls, which uniformly show that the public is fed up with the rising tide of sex, violence, and vulgarity in the entertainment media. These surveys are useful, but based on my conversations with people in diners, schools, and small businesses back in Connecticut, I believe they barely begin to measure the public's intense feelings toward television.

My experience tells me that beneath the surface of the Telecommunications Revolution bubbles a revolution of another kind—a "Revolt of the Revolted," as author William Bennett and I have taken to calling it. It is being fueled by a growing sense that our culture is not only out of touch with the values of mainstream America, but out of control as well. Many people believe that there are no standards that television will not violate, no lines television will not cross. Broadcasters may see the V-chip as a threat to their independence and financial well-being, but many average citizens see television as a threat to their children and their country. In the V-chip, they perceive a modicum of protection for their families.

Why are people afraid of television? Much of the news media has focused on the violence, but that is only part of the problem. Millions of Americans are fed up with explicit sex scenes and crude language during prime time and with the pornographic content of those abysmal talk shows and soap operas during the day. They feel television is not only offensive, but on the offensive, assaulting the values they and most of their neighbors share.

People are angry because they cannot sit down to watch TV with their children without fearing they will be embarrassed or demeaned. And they are angry because they feel our culture has been hijacked and replaced with something alien to their lives, something that openly rejects rather than reflects the values they try to instill in their families. In the world they see on TV, sex is a recreational pastime, indecency is a cause for laughter, and humans are killed as casually and senselessly as bugs. It is a coarse caricature of the America they love. . . .

This is a very anxious time in our history. The bonds of trust that people once took for granted in their neighborhoods and schools and workplaces are withering, and the social order that once anchored their lives and their communities is breaking apart. Stability is giving way to an increasingly chaotic and threatening world. . . .

The source of this social breakdown, many people believe, is the collapse of fundamental values. A critical connection exists between the erosion of morals and the explosion of social pathologies around us—brutal violence committed more and more often by strangers, the disintegration of the family, the epidemic of illegitimacy. In much the same way, many of us see a critical link between this erosion of values and the plummeting standards of decency on television and in our culture.

THE MEDIA AND SOCIAL PROBLEMS

Some in the entertainment industry continue to argue that they are merely holding up a mirror to our culture, and scoff at the notion that the entertainment culture is responsible for all our social ills. The time has come to take a torch to this straw man.

Neither President Clinton nor William Bennett nor I nor anyone I know is suggesting that any individual entertainment product, or even the whole of the entertainment industry, has single-handedly caused the rise in juvenile violence or illegitimacy. We are saying that the entertainment culture is immensely powerful, more powerful than any lawmaker in Washington, and that this power is wielded in ways that make our country's problems worse, not better.

Reprinted by permission of Jerry Barnett for the *Indianapolis News*.

Consider a few facts. There are 95 million households in America with televisions, which means more households own TV sets than telephones. Sixty-five percent of those homes have at least two TVs, which on average are turned on seven hours a day. The typical child watches 25 hours of television every week. That is more time than most of them spend attending religious services, talking to their parents, reading books, or even listening to their teachers. Many kids spend more time watching television than any other activity except sleeping.

No one can seriously deny the potential influence that kind of constant exposure carries with it. And because of that power, those responsible for television programming do not just mirror, but also mold, attitudes and behaviors. Whether they want the responsibility or not, they are influencing our values. And whenever they air degrading programs, they contribute to—not cause, but contribute to—the moral and social breakdown we are suffering.

So many studies have documented the threat posed by steady exposure to violence on television that the point should not even be subject to debate. But to add yet another voice to the mix, consider this passage from a stunning article Adam Walinsky wrote in 1995 in the *Atlantic Monthly*, in which he warned of a coming generation of "superfelons" who when they mature will likely make the cities of today look peaceful:

> These young people have been raised in the glare of ceaseless media violence and incitement to every depravity of act and spirit. Movies may feature scores of killings in two hours' time, vying to show methods ever more horrific. . . . Major corporations make and sell records exhorting their listeners to brutalize Koreans, rob store owners, rape women, kill police. . . . These lessons are being taught to millions of children as I write and you read.

The media's messages are not transforming these young people into killers, Walinsky says, but they are feeding into a cycle of violence that is getting harder and harder to break and that has dire repercussions for our country. Much the same could be said about the effect of sexual messages sent to our children. . . .

If you still doubt the influence that television wields, just listen to America's parents. I cannot tell you how many times I've heard mothers and fathers say that they feel locked in a struggle with the powerful forces of the electronic culture to shape their children's values—and that they're losing. They feel that television and the culture undermine their fundamental duty as a parent—teaching right and wrong, instilling a sense of discipline—and that their kids' lives are increasingly controlled by careless strangers a world away.

THE V-CHIP AND ITS LIMITS

This is why the concept of the V-chip is so appealing to parents. It offers them a silicon hard hat to protect their kids from television's falling standards. The implications of the V-chip's popularity are remarkable. The public feels so strongly that their children need to be shielded from words and images in the entertainment media that they are turning to the government for help—not censorship, but help. Considering the low esteem with which Americans today regard Washington, this should tell us something about the public's faith and trust in the TV industry. . . .

To their credit, the networks and the National Association of Broadcasters dropped their opposition [to the V-chip] following the president's appeal in his State of the Union address and agreed (albeit reluctantly) to create a comprehensive, self-enforced rating system. Regardless of how it came to pass, this was a historic breakthrough. The tools offered by the V-chip and a ratings system will go a long way toward empowering parents to keep overly violent and offensive programs out of their homes and out of reach of their children.

But the industry must realize that these tools will not eliminate the fundamental problem that is fueling the deep-seated anger felt by so many Americans: the deterioration of the industry's programming standards. The V-chip is no panacea; the harmful messages abounding on television are still going to reach many young kids. Moreover, the V-chip is no substitute for network responsibility, for recognizing that the programming they send into our homes carries with it enormous influence. Simply put, the American public wants more from television than just good warnings on bad programming.

There is some reason for hope. A growing chorus of voices within the industry is calling for fundamental changes in the way television does business. For instance, in a high-profile speech, Richard Frank, the president of the Academy of Television Arts and Sciences, recently said, "Why do you think people such as C. Delores Tucker, William Bennett, Tipper Gore, Reed Hundt and many others are attacking music and the media? Because *the reality is frightening*" (emphasis added). Frank went on to urge the industry to use the enormous power at its disposal to take some risks and set higher standards. "We cannot and will not ignore the important issues facing television," he said. "We must deal with them responsibly."

A CODE OF CONDUCT

One of the most important steps the industry can take now to address the concerns we have raised, and to begin to restore public confidence in its programming, would be to adopt once again a voluntary code of conduct. I know that some in the creative community will charge that such a code is an attempt to chill their free speech, but the truth is that self-regulation is common sense, not censorship.

The time has come to recognize that not every aberrant behavior or hostile voice has the right to be featured on television on a daily basis, especially at times when large numbers of children are watching. That means asking the industry to draw some lines which programmers cannot and will not cross, something Court TV has already done by adopting a code of ethics for its own programming.

I hope that the industry will include in any voluntary code they develop a commitment to bring back the Family Hour and to recreate a safe haven for children during prime time. The major broadcast networks would not only be helping parents by taking this step, they would also be helping themselves. There clearly is a market for high-quality, family-friendly material, as evidenced by the fact that Nickelodeon was the top-rated cable network in the nation in 1995. This channel has viewers that ABC, NBC, CBS, and Fox could win back. . . .

THE BIG PICTURE

These are just a few suggestions. The devil here is not in the details but in the big picture—or rather, in all the troubling pictures and words the TV industry is pumping into our homes, and in the damage that the sum of those messages inflicts upon our society. The people who run television have a choice before them: Respond to this Revolt of the Revolted, or face the Sentinels of Censorship. The last thing I want is the government setting standards, but I fear the public will soon turn again to Congress to take stronger actions if the TV industry continues on its path downward.

We must avoid that outcome at all costs. To do so, the TV industry must see the V-chip for the powerful symbol of discontent it is, and treat it as a beginning and not an end. More and more these days television is becoming a pariah in America's living rooms, and no slice of silicone can block out that reality.

"Media literacy education is a fresh and valuable contribution to ultimately reducing the depiction of violence on television and in the media."

MEDIA LITERACY EDUCATION CAN ADDRESS THE PROBLEM OF MEDIA VIOLENCE

Elizabeth Thoman

In the following viewpoint, taken from testimony before a U.S. Senate committee, Elizabeth Thoman argues that media literacy education can be an effective antidote to the negative social effects of media violence. She advocates programs that teach students of all ages to critically view and assess the media images they perceive, to distinguish between real and staged violence, and to make informed choices about what they read, hear, and see. Such education, Thoman asserts, will counteract the harmful lessons she believes many television programs teach about violence. In addition, she contends, media literacy education could raise future public support for reforms in America's mass media institutions that might reduce the amount of media violence they produce. Thoman is the founder and director of the Center for Media Literacy, a Los Angeles, California–based nonprofit organization that produces teacher training and community education materials designed to promote media literacy.

As you read, consider the following questions:

1. What is the "circle of blame" that Thoman describes?
2. What is Thoman's definition of media literacy?
3. According to the author, what important question underlies the debate over violent images in the media?

Reprinted from Elizabeth Thoman's testimony in *Television Violence*, a hearing before the U.S. Senate Committee on Commerce, Science, and Transportation, July 12, 1995.

For 40 years, the American people have been engaged in a "circle of blame" about media violence. Here's how it works:

Viewers, particularly parents, concerned for their children about something they see on television or in the media, blame those who write and create the shows.

Writers/directors say it's the producers who require violence in programs in order to get them financed.

Producers blame *corporate executives* for demanding "action" in order to get ratings.

Corporate executives say competition is brutal and blame the advertisers for pulling out unless a show gets high ratings.

Advertisers say it's all up to the *viewers!*

It's time to stop the circle of blame and recognize we all share responsibility for the culture we are creating and passing on to our children. It is very important that we consider a variety of solutions to this issue. *There is no one solution.* But among the efforts being presented here today, I believe that media literacy education is a fresh and valuable contribution to ultimately reducing the depiction of violence on television and in the media.

DEFINING MEDIA LITERACY

What is media literacy?

Media literacy, as defined in a 1992 report from the Aspen Institute, is the movement "to expand notions of literacy to include the powerful post-print media that dominate our informational landscape." We define the media literate person as one who can "access, understand, analyze, and communicate messages in a variety of forms." Call it "driver's training for the information highway." In any case, we are talking about a new vision of literacy for the 21st century.

The media literacy movement actually encompasses three stages on a continuum of what we might call a "media empowerment movement."

The first stage is learning to *balance or manage one's media "diet."* Just as we teach children good eating habits, we must also teach our children good viewing habits that they can take into adulthood and, ultimately, share with their own children. This stage requires parent education, of course, and programs are beginning to be conducted by the parent-teacher association (PTA), parent education programs, churches and others. For many parents, it's also the *motivational training* that will be needed to help them understand that, like it or not, *managing media in their children's lives* is an essential part of parenting today. Such motivational training may also be a necessary step for some parents to purchase and use any kind of blocking or monitoring device.

The second stage is learning *specific skills of critical viewing*—that is, learning to analyze and question what is on the screen, how it is constructed and what may have been left out. This is the task of more formal media literacy classes in schools and after-school programs for children and teens as well as in adult education opportunities for grown-ups of all ages.

The third stage we call critical or social analysis. It explores deeper issues of how mass media makes meaning in society and drives the consumer economy, that is, who produces the media we experience—and for what purpose? What are the political, economic and social forces that converge to shape the cultural environment in which we live our lives? This stage also questions whether our mass media system can or should be different. This more philosophical stage will not be engaged in by everyone, but it is necessary for informed and responsible media activism or what I call "citizenship in a media culture.". . .

With that brief overview, let me address specifically how media literacy applies to the current problem we are facing in our media about depictions of violence.

THE WRONG QUESTION

For those same 40 years the circle of blame I mentioned earlier has been fueled by one unanswerable question: "Does watching violence cause someone to become violent?" Or as the talk shows might put it: Does TV kill?

The reason we've gotten nowhere on this issue for 40 years is because this is the wrong question to ask about violence in the media.

It's a limiting question because it focuses the impact of media only on single individuals rather than a more diffuse impact on larger communities which are, of course, made up of individuals but which also have their own cultural "environment" that is larger than any one individual.

According to the American Psychological Association's (APA) 1993 report, *Violence and Youth: Psychology's Response,* there are actually four long term effects of viewing violence:

1. Increased aggressiveness and anti-social behavior.
   (This may not just be becoming an ax-murderer. It can also mean increased arrests for domestic violence and child abuse, drunk driving, even an "in your face" attitude about the world.)
2. Increased fear of being or becoming a victim.

(The "mean world syndrome" / creating a self-perpetuating prison of paranoia)
3. Increased desensitization to violence and victims of violence. (Loss of "Good Samaritan" ethic and a fundamental principle of democratic societies: building the common good)
4. Increased appetite for more and more violence in entertainment and real life.
(The ability to tolerate more violent media and to engage in increasingly risky or dangerous behaviors)

DEVELOPING CRITICAL-THINKING SKILLS

The best way to help children deal with violent television is to watch with them and talk to them about what they see. Find out what they understand and what they don't. Media-literacy curricula provide a variety of tools to help parents and children analyze the techniques used to stage violent scenes and decode the various depictions of violence in different media genres—news, cartoons, drama, sports, and music. It is important for children to learn the difference between reality and fantasy at an early age and to know how costumes, camera angles, and special effects can fool them.

Don't simply say to kids, "Violence is bad for you and you shouldn't watch it." Instead, encourage them to develop an awareness of violence when they see it and understand its consequences through their own experience. Critical-thinking skills will stay with kids when you can't be there. Through guided practice, critical viewing can become an everyday habit for both children and adults.

Elizabeth Thoman, *Better Viewing*, May/June 1995.

If we consider all four effects and reflect on everyday life in current society, we will surely agree with the APA that "Even those who do not themselves increase their violent behaviors are significantly affected by their viewing of violence."

To reduce the issue of media violence to "does TV kill?" trivializes a very complex question that faces our global society on the brink of the 21st century. The real question should be: *What is the long-term impact on our national psyche when millions of children, in their formative years, grow up decade after decade bombarded with very powerful visual and verbal messages demonstrating violence as the way to solve problems?*

THE LARGER QUESTION

Actually there's even a larger question here than just the question of the portrayal of violent images on TV and in the media.

The much larger question is:

- *What kind of culture, what kind of psychological environment do we want our children to grow up in?*

- And then, when we achieve some consensus on that, we can further decide what is the role and responsibility of mass communications and technology (among many other factors) in contributing to that cultural, that mental environment.

The Center for Media Literacy believes that to engage this question is to explore a fundamental issue of our time. But we need it to happen not just in political speeches or talk shows or even academic forums. We need to enroll millions of Americans in what we might call a "national conversation" to resolve the issue of media violence in their own lives and ultimately in our common society. This is not as difficult as it might seem.

PEOPLE WANT INFORMATION

All across America, every day, and into the night, there are classes in schools and colleges, discussion groups in church basements and public libraries and Rotary clubs. There are after-school programs for teen-agers and elderhostels for senior citizens. People of all ages are hungry for relevant information that can help them cope with the stresses of living today. *I propose that media literacy education is a valuable and critical tool for learning to navigate our way through the sea of information and images that make up our modern media-saturated society.*

Perhaps violence has proliferated in our mass entertainment culture because citizens haven't had the information they need to make truly informed choices. In the past 20 years, we've learned to make different choices around smoking and cholesterol and buckling up your seatbelt. Media literacy proposes that, with different information, viewers might make different choices or engage in different behaviors.

There is clear evidence that skills of media literacy can be taught to even young children and they can have an impact on a child's ability to apply critical thinking to a variety of media. Does that mean they will never watch Power Rangers again? Not necessarily. But I guarantee they'll never watch it passively or without thinking again—and that alone can make a huge difference! . . .

THE PROMISE OF MEDIA LITERACY

Media literacy education is, I believe, a fundamental step in the long-term "de-marketing" of violence as a commodity in our culture.

I have no doubt that when millions of Americans have the

opportunity to examine the many issues around media violence and practice skills of media advocacy and action, . . . we will see a dramatic increase in the public opinion and strategic actions that will slowly, but surely, yield changes in our media system. Because it is an educational process and not a "quick fix" solution, media literacy may not make the headlines today. But it will influence the media world our children will inherit tomorrow. This is what counts.

Periodical Bibliography

The following articles have been selected to supplement the diverse views presented in this chapter. Addresses are provided for periodicals not indexed in the *Readers' Guide to Periodical Literature*, the *Alternative Press Index*, the *Social Sciences Index*, or the *Index to Legal Periodicals and Books*.

William S. Abbott — "To Reduce TV Violence," *Christian Social Action*, June 1994. Available from 100 Maryland Ave. NE, Washington, DC 20002.

Stephen Baker — "The Right Spot for the Idiot Box," *Business Week*, April 29, 1996.

Ginia Bellafante — "So What's On in Tokyo?" *Time*, February 19, 1996.

Bert Briller — "No Answer to Violence . . . or Are There Many Answers?" *Television Quarterly*, vol. 27, no. 4, 1995.

Education Digest — "TV Violence and Kids," Spring 1996.

Mark Hoerrner — "The Good, the Bad, and the Ugly: Homeschoolers Show Parental Involvement Is the Key to Curbing Television Violence," *Home Education Magazine*, November/December 1996. Available from PO Box 1083, Tonasket, WA 98855.

D.E. Levin and N. Carlsson-Paige — "Disempowering the 'Power Rangers,'" *Education Digest*, May 1996.

Madeline Levine — "Handling the 'Boo Tube,'" *Parents*, October 1996.

Suzanne Braun Levine — "Caution: Children Watching," *Ms.*, July/August 1994.

Roger Mahony — "God and Hollywood," *New Perspectives Quarterly*, Spring 1995.

Mary Megee — "Media Literacy: The New Basic," *Education Digest*, September 1997.

Sara Rimer — "With TV Off, Real Life Reasserts Itself," *New York Times*, May 1, 1996.

Rosalind Silver — "Challenging the Myths of Media Violence," *Television Quarterly*, vol. 27, no. 2, 1994.

USA Today — "Youths Not Convinced by Anti-Violence Ads," August 1996.

U.S. News & World Report — "What TV-Savvy Parents Can Do to Help Their Kids," September 11, 1995.

DOES MEDIA VIOLENCE HAVE ARTISTIC VALUE?

CHAPTER PREFACE

In May 1995, Senator Robert Dole of Kansas created national headlines for a speech in which he assailed the Hollywood film industry for producing gruesomely violent scenes and other "nightmares of depravity." In some respects, his attack was nothing new; rather, it was a continuation of a long tradition of public debate over the violent (and sexual) content of motion pictures—a debate with both moral and aesthetic overtones.

This debate goes back as far as the 1920s and 1930s, when growing numbers of Americans expressed concern about the violent, risqué, and lawless behavior displayed in motion pictures. To forestall possible government regulation, the film industry established the Motion Picture Producers and Distributors of America (MPPDA), appointed former postmaster general Will H. Hays as the association's head, and enacted a production code. Strengthened in 1934, the MPPDA code banned brutality, gore, cruelty to children and animals, stories featuring revenge killing, and depictions of crimes that could be imitated, such as murder, arson, and robbery. A motion picture could not be distributed without the "Hays" seal of approval. This code remained in force until 1968, when it was replaced by an age-based ratings system that is still in use today.

Film critics and others have long debated the merits and legacy of the Hays system. Some believe that the years in which the code was in operation constitute Hollywood's "golden age." The increasingly explicit depictions of violence found in movies since 1968, they argue, have little to offer in terms of artistic value or entertainment. But others assert that motion picture creators, free of code restrictions, now have greater artistic freedom to create realistic and powerful motion pictures. Many memorable motion pictures with violent themes have been made in the years since the code was abolished, they contend.

While few Americans would call for a return to the Hays era, many wonder if the pendulum has not swung too far toward the other extreme. In the following chapter, authors debate whether violence enriches or debases motion pictures and television programs.

| "Television violence can and should be defended."

TELEVISION VIOLENCE HAS ARTISTIC VALUE

David Link

Most criticism of television violence, notes David Link in the following viewpoint, has been directed at fictional violence rather than the real-life violence shown in news or sports programs. Link, a writer who lives in Los Angeles, defends the fictional violence found on television, contending that it is almost always presented in a moral context that condemns rather than glorifies violence. Violence has been an important theme of storytelling in art and literature since the time of the ancient Greek tragedies, he asserts, because people share a fundamental need to explore all aspects of the human condition. Link criticizes political efforts to censor or limit violence on television, arguing that adults should not be treated as helpless children unable to cope with or learn from television violence.

As you read, consider the following questions:

1. What consensus have Americans reached about television violence, according to Link?
2. What distinction does the author make between fictional violence and the violence found in nonfiction news programming?
3. Why do people find violence so fascinating, in Link's opinion?

As the debate over violence on television plods forward, TV's critics seem to have achieved a decided advantage—they have virtually no opposition. Everybody decries TV violence. Nobody even plays devil's advocate. Some people have tangentially answered the critics by bringing up the First Amendment and censorship. But that's as far as it's gone. No one defends violence on television. And when Americans all line up on one side of an issue, you know something is terribly, terribly wrong.

I write fiction. While the focus of my dramatic writing has been theater and movies, like most Americans I watch television. And I think television violence can and should be defended. The problem isn't that people pay too much attention to the violence that appears on television; the problem is they pay too little.

DEBATE ABOUT FICTION

To begin, this is a debate about fiction. We are far too much in love with the real-life violence on television to want to do anything about it. Televised football, boxing, and hockey not only depict violence, they have physical conflict as their primary purpose. And real-life violence dominates TV news: Murder, robbery, drive-by shootings, fires, death, injury accidents on the freeway—all are guaranteed their place on the news whenever they occur, and the more horrendous the circumstances, the more heated the coverage. Whether or not the news actually shows the bullet pass through the body, as occurred when the Telemundo network's cameras captured a man murdering his ex-wife at a cemetery, is irrelevant. The thing that draws us to these stories time after time is the fact of violence, violence's explicit or implicit presence. When Phil Donahue or Oprah or 60 Minutes or PrimeTime Live tells us about Lorena Bobbitt cutting off her husband's genitals, we lean a little closer to the set and toy with the images being conjured.

This is not necessarily bad. It is hard to argue that we shouldn't know or talk about the real violence that occurs in society, its causes, and its consequences. And the drawing power of violent sports speaks for itself. That leaves only fictional violence as the target of this debate. It's much easier to maintain that fiction writers, who by definition make things up, should make up less that includes the depiction of violence.

But what is it everyone's getting so exercised about? Of all the popular dramatic forms, television is by far the least violent. . . . On the whole, television today is less violent than it has been in more than a quarter of a century.

Television is the subject of the current controversy not because it is the most violent medium but because it is the most vulnerable. In 1978, the Supreme Court held in *FCC v. Pacifica Foundation* that broadcast media that come into the home are not entitled to the same First Amendment protection other art forms enjoy. While the reasoning in that case has undergone some serious erosion in recent years (and, in the thinking of some, wasn't too steady to begin with), it remains the vehicle that Attorney General Janet Reno and others ride in their crusade. And it is a vehicle that is seriously overloaded.

Part of a Story

The problem is that we assume televised, fictional violence is the same as the implicit or explicit violence that is the subject of nonfiction news. But there is a critical difference between the two. When television journalists report the latest carjacking or the murder of a 6-year-old, the report is singular, disjointed, one report among others that bear no relation to one another except that for that day someone has decided that they constitute "news." Even on a magazine show such as 20/20, stories can be given only 10 or 12 minutes of air time, not enough to tell them in a fully developed context. Compare this to fiction, where every event, including every act of violence, is presented as part of a whole story. There is a beginning to the story, a middle to it, and an end.

That fact, almost always left out of this debate, has consequences. When we see a complete story, we are given the material to make judgments about the characters and their actions. Every story has some message, every writer has an intention, and most reasonable fiction writers expect their audiences to make judgments. While such judgments are possible with nonfiction, we also know that a news report is not complete, that the news crew could only capture a certain amount of the story's context for presentation in a restricted forum with next to no time for elaboration.

In the debate over television violence, too many people are ripping fictional acts of violence from the context their stories provide, as though viewers were watching those acts as isolated incidents on the 6 o'clock news. A recent ad by the American Family Association laments that by the time a child has finished elementary school, he or she will have witnessed 8,000 murders and more than 100,000 acts of violence on television. These figures appear to indicate that a lot of fictional acts of violence have appeared on television, at least in the past. (Or that the definition of "act of violence" is so broad it is almost meaningless, but that's another argument.) What the figures leave out is the context in which those acts occurred.

A Moral Context

Consider the argument, brought out like a trusty musket, that fiction too often "glorifies" violence. The truth is that it does not. On television in particular, the overwhelming number of violent acts are committed by someone clearly identifiable as an antagonist. In cases where a protagonist engages in violence, that violence is either legitimized by justice or righteousness, or it is a necessary response to a violent provocation. In every one of those three situations—antagonist violence; protagonist violence to accomplish justice; or protagonist violence in defense of self or others, and to which there is no reasonable alternative—the act falls well short of "glorification."

It is hard even in motion pictures and theater to find examples in which violence is glorified. The touchstone is probably Stanley Kubrick's *A Clockwork Orange*. In that film, the most brutal violence is accompanied by seductive, humorous, or lush music; it is choreographed like a ballet. More important, when the state removes the violent impulses of Alex, the main character, the audience is lured into rooting for the procedure to fail. At the end, when it does fail, there is a sense of relief that Alex has returned to normal.

Violence Can Teach Ethical Lessons

To a free and democratic republic such as the United States, the depiction of violence is not frightening in the least, since it reflects a fundamental confidence in individual freedom and personal liberty. Repeated illustrations of violence and immorality are necessary to impart ethical lessons to the citizenry just as "hellfire and brimstone" are used in sermons to emphasize the frightening prospect of hell. Likewise, acts of violence are often the means of resisting evil. Those who believe in "nonviolent conflict resolution" by highly paid "facilitators" have no use for a Clint Eastwood or a Ronald Reagan who says: "Make my day" and means it.

Laurence Jarvik, *Insight*, December 19, 1994.

This turns conventional morality about violence upside-down, the very point of the film. For purposes of the present debate, though, *A Clockwork Orange* illustrates an attitude toward violence that is so rare as to be almost nonexistent, especially on television. Television violence is nearly always presented in the conventional moral framework. When an antagonist commits an act of violence, it is clear that it is wrong. When a protagonist commits an act of violence, it is either morally good, because it accomplishes justice, or it is morally questionable, regrettable but, as a defensive act, necessary to preserve some greater good. There are no Alexes on television.

Even on *Beavis and Butt-head*, any fair reading is that their violent acts are committed by vacuous losers, Dead-End Kids for the '90s, and in that context violence is not "glorified" or intended to be a model for behavior. Beavis and Butt-head may be violent, but they are also terminally bored, Samuel Beckett meets Hanna-Barbera. Boredom is their entire context. Compare *Beavis and Butt-head* to *The Itchy & Scratchy Show*, which occasionally appears on *The Simpsons*. *Itchy & Scratchy* is a macabre, ghastly look at the way we used to present violence to children, but its violence is so far over the top that it is impossible to miss the satire. Beavis and Butt-head don't revel in their violence the way Itchy and Scratchy do; they don't revel in anything. That's the point. While *Beavis and Butt-head* involves a more attenuated morality than the obvious satire of *Itchy & Scratchy*, if viewers see any of these characters as role models, they are thoroughly misreading the shows.

CONVENTIONAL ATTITUDES

Even in the movies shown on television, conventional attitudes about violence predominate. There is a number of movies that are over-full of violence; teen slasher movies and martial arts films are the most obvious examples. But far more often than not, movies do not stray too far from the conventional moral framework that condemns rather than exalts any act of violence. Movies that do violate the expected moral framework about violence, or that come close to the line (*Bad Lieutenant*), will generally not make it to television.

A good example of the violence that does make it to television is the 1987 feature film, *Predator*, starring Arnold Schwarzenegger. It was recently shown on a Sunday afternoon, a time when young children would likely be watching. By any measure, there is a tremendous amount of violence in this film, in which Schwarzenegger is called for duty to rescue a VIP whose plane has gone down in a hostile jungle and winds up having to fend off one of the most disagreeable aliens ever to hit the screen.

While there is far more violence in *Predator* than in *A Clockwork Orange*, Schwarzenegger's film puts violence in a context that cannot be missed. That context, shared with most violent films, is a question: What is the response to the violence in the world? Schwarzenegger's Dutch uses violence reluctantly; he even chastises his co-star, Carl Weathers, who in one scene is too eager to confront violence with violence. But at film's end, it is Dutch against the alien, only one of them will survive, and only the most intentionally perverse viewer would root for the alien. Dutch hews to a reasonably clear moral line about violence, using it either when it will accomplish justice (the script's inciting incident is an attempt to rescue innocent people who went down in the plane and are being held hostage) or ultimately for self-preservation. In the world the movie presents, Dutch or others would die if he were not violent. People living in South-Central L.A. might understand that world view; Korean grocers do.

THE DRAWING POWER OF VIOLENCE

Some movies do focus obsessively and crassly on violence. And some of these movies make it to TV, or at least cable. *Predator* could have been made with fewer explosions, less blood, less explicitness. But it is here that the argument against violence on television breaks down most seriously. No one can deny that young children or even turbulent adolescents or vulnerable adults might stumble on such a movie and become transfixed. The question is, Why? The American Family Association is right that over the years we can see thousands and thousands of individual acts of violence on television. But anyone who sees a televised movie that exploits violence and who then decides violence is "cool" has to reject the thousands upon thousands of hours of television's moral lessons to the contrary, has to be entirely immune to the context in which cautious producers present even excessive violence time after time after time.

Even the strongest emotional argument used by violence's critics loses its force if context is seriously considered. Assuming that too many children are raised by parents who do not teach them a clear rejection of violence, what forces would cause even the most vulnerable viewers to reject the repeated message from television that violence is at best a necessary but questionable solution, but is more often outright wrong? The power of violence must be so overwhelming that moral lessons to the contrary are irrelevant.

And maybe that's true. Anyone with any historical perspective knows that violence appears to be an eternal theme, from Homer and the Bible right up to Schwarzenegger and Sylvester Stallone. Despite millennia of moral teachings to the contrary, some people are going to murder, rape, mutilate, and torture others, and there seems to be no certain way to predict who will, or to prevent them from doing so. But violence continues to be a story—both on the news and in drama—because it is unusual, something the vast majority of people do not engage in.

The drawing power of violence is not television's fault, any more than it is the Bible's. Anyone who has actually read the Bible is well aware of the grisly, explicit, and hideous scenes of violence that are sometimes recounted there, acts even the crassest producer would never dream of presenting on television. Yet the Bible is known for its moral teachings, while television's moral teachings about violence, which are wholly consistent with much of the Bible, are viewed as nonexistent, no matter how often and regularly they are repeated. Those people who engage in violent acts in real life have ignored what they have seen on television, not given it too much credence.

CALLS FOR MORAL INSTRUCTION

What politicians and activists are now demanding from fiction is something law and religion have been unable to accomplish in centuries of trying: moral instruction that people will uniformly follow. While moral condemnations of art go back for centuries, the stakes have now grown because of the pervasiveness of television. In the present debate, Janet Reno has given dark but unmistakable hints that if artists don't voluntarily do something to stop this "national epidemic of violence," Washington will have to step in. In this Reno follows the Greek philosopher Plato, who long ago concluded: "Both poets and prose-writers tell bad tales about men in most important matters; they say that many unjust men are happy and many just men wretched, that injustice is profitable if it escapes notice, that justice is another's good and one's own punishment. I think we will forbid these tales and order them to compose the opposite kind of poetry and tell the opposite kind of tales."

Two premises underlie this desire to regulate art. First is the assumption that audiences are incapable of serious reflection and will mindlessly imitate what is presented to them. Second is that they will imitate good actions only when no bad actions are presented to the contrary. These assumptions may be an appropriate way to deal with young children. As some recent studies have confirmed, the sappy happiness of the purple dinosaur Barney, while cloying to many adults, provides very young children with a needed center. But such premises make no sense when dealing with adults.

And particularly when television is concerned, there is no rational way to separate adult audiences from younger audiences. There is no way to ensure that all parents will have their young children in bed by 9 or 10 p.m., and since children might be exposed to television accidentally at any given moment (and a moment is all it takes, at least the way this debate is shaping up), television must be wiped clean of all violence, of any bad action someone might imitate. There's no telling which child will be the one to imitate some fleeting image. Those on the P.C. [political correctness] watch will note that in this argument the culture of victimization reaches its nadir: Because of the vulnerability of a few, everybody must be treated like a child. In this scenario, everyone is a victim—a victim of art.

What Reno, like Plato, wants from artists is not art, it is edification. Art, by its nature, deals with complexity. The raw material of great drama is not answers but questions. Human interactions are fascinating precisely because they are enigmatic. The scene in Disney's film *The Program* in which young men lie down in the middle of the road was compelling because every adolescent male understands testing the limits, taking the dare. In this, the scene fits into a long tradition: *Rebel Without a Cause*'s game of chicken, for example, or *Stand By Me*'s bridge-crossing scene. It is tragic that boys died by imitating the scene from Disney's film. But the reason they imitated it is the same reason it was presented—because it was fascinating.

VIOLENCE AND HUMAN NATURE

Such reasons are located deep within human nature. The illogic of violence has been a theme in literature from its beginnings with Homer, was exploited to great effect in Greek tragedy, brought explicitly to life in the hundreds of revenge plays that peppered the English Renaissance, and continues to fascinate in works as varied as Woody Allen's *Crimes and Misdemeanors*, Joseph Heller's *Catch-22*, and the recent television movie, *A Mother's Revenge*, which, while fictional, reverberates with the story of Ellie Nessler, who, frustrated with the justice system, shot and killed the man who had molested her child. We know that violence is wrong, everything around us reinforces that conviction, and yet sometimes we become violent. Why do humans act irrationally? That was Mr. Spock's eternal question in *Star Trek*, it is the question that lurks in every romantic comedy or murder mystery, and it is the grain of sand that irritates and motivates those of us who make up stories. If everyone acted logically, if everyone followed the rules, we wouldn't need fiction, and George Orwell's

1984 would make no sense. It is the defiance in us that fascinates, not the compliance.

What is really at issue here is the war within human nature, the conflicts between what we know to be the law and what we feel. That theme has been explicit at least since *Antigone*. Sometimes the law is wrong, or does not adequately address an individual situation. And sometimes an individual feels compelled to go outside the law, even though objectively doing so is harmful. Thus, when the mother shoots her child's rapist in *A Mother's Revenge*, the script clearly portrays that deed as wrong, and yet it is an action the audience can understand. The question, "What would you do?" was prominent in the advertising for that movie. The point of the film was not to "answer" the question of revenge but to pose it, explore it. The story does not promote violence, glorify violence, or condemn violence. It is merely about violence.

VIOLENCE IS A TOOL

Violence and danger are among the tools I have as a fiction maker, alongside sex, religion, truth, authority, honor, and every other human characteristic—strengths and weaknesses alike. Individually and in combination these characteristics can have tremendous effect, can lead people to laughter, outrage, understanding, compassion. But as tools, they have no value until they are used. Homer and Shakespeare, Francis Ford Coppola and Martin Scorsese have used the tool of violence well to tell us some fundamental truths about ourselves. Many more have used violence poorly.

Aristotle said centuries ago that tragedy seeks to evoke pity and terror in the audience. This is as true now as it ever was. And something inside us wants pity and terror from more than just drama. Political campaigns are regularly about pity and terror, the daily news is about pity and terror, gossip is about pity and terror, gross-out contests among 10-year-olds are about pity and terror. Whatever the source of that need, it is fundamental to human nature, and somehow human nature always provides abundant stories, real or imagined, to supply the need.

The answer to television violence is not to treat adults like children but to recognize that children are capable of learning the lessons they will need as adults. Parents must teach their children at an early age that they are supposed to read television the same way they read a book—with care for the meaning. None of us is simple, so you must constantly read between the lines, verify what we say against your values and truths. Only then can you decide how to take what we say, to believe us, follow us, or condemn us.

Unless we learn to read the stories we are told better than we have been, we will continue to argue over nothing and to blame artists for problems that reside at the heart of human nature. If we use the recent, unfortunate incidents involving children and reckless adolescents to justify artistic regulation, we risk taking the beauty and greatness out of art. We will have to forbid artists to write about human beings. What we will leave behind is a tepid trail of catechisms for simpletons, bloodless tales no one would have any desire to watch in the first place, much less imitate.

"The fact is, whatever may be the case with sex or violence in serious artistic media, everybody knows that they are always gratuitous on television."

TELEVISION VIOLENCE HAS NO ARTISTIC VALUE

James Bowman

James Bowman is the American editor of the London *Times Literary Supplement* and film critic for the *American Spectator* magazine. In the following viewpoint, Bowman takes issue with those who maintain that some depictions of violence on television have artistic merit. Unlike theater or other serious artistic media, the overriding goal of commercial television is to deliver an audience to advertisers, he states. Thus, television does not use violence as a means toward creating art, Bowman contends, but instead depends on scenes of explicit violence (as well as sexual and suggestive material) to attract and titillate viewers and make a profit for the networks.

As you read, consider the following questions:

1. What opinions does Bowman express about the arguments made by people in the television industry who say they are fighting for free speech rights?
2. What is the difference between such works as the motion picture *Schindler's List*, which includes violent and nude scenes, and standard television fare, according to Bowman?
3. What solution does the author implicitly suggest for parents concerned about the impact of television on their children?

Reprinted from James Bowman, "Overrating TV," *The New Criterion*, September 1997, by permission of *The New Criterion*.

N ot sex 'n' violence again! But they're so boring! Or at least the endless, po-faced discussions of how or whether they may be kept off television would be boring if it were not for the ludicrous public spectacle they afford. On the one side is the inevitably comic Grundyism of those who devote their lives to counting up the number of times someone says the word *ass* in the family hour of prime time (twenty-nine times in the month of February 1997, according to Thomas Johnson of the Parents' Television Council); on the other side is the nauseating hypocrisy involved in the cash-engorged television networks' striking attitudes as idealistic defenders of free speech. It is a farce which pushes that of the complementary priggeries of pro- and anti-tobacco forces off the stage.

THE RATINGS SYSTEM

Now, however, all the huffing and puffing have produced a concrete result. As of October 1, 1997, the voluntary ratings system for network television shows, in effect only since the beginning of the year, will be supplemented with additional information, about the "intensity" and frequency of offensive material, designed to help parents more finely to calibrate their regulation of their children's television viewing habits. The networks fiercely resisted any amendments to the age-based rating system—devised in 1996 with the help of Jack Valenti, the head of the Motion Picture Association of America who designed a similar system for the movies back in the 1960s. But this system had come under such withering criticism from would-be congressional regulators and parent and children advocacy groups that all except NBC finally accepted an emended version of it in July 1997.

In return, their congressional critics, led by Representative Edwin Markey of Massachusetts, have agreed to a three-year moratorium on new legislation concerning program content. Many of the advocacy groups and some strongly anti-smut legislators, including senators Joseph Lieberman of Connecticut and Sam Brownback of Kansas, considered this a corrupt bargain and refused to be bound by Markey's promise. There has also very recently been a strong movement in the House of Representatives, to which the Speaker gave his support, to bring back the "family hour" by law. But there does appear to be a good chance that Representative Markey's moratorium will hold, at least until it becomes clear how, or if, the so-called "V-chip," due to be installed in new television sets from 1998, is working.

The original ratings system introduced at the beginning of 1997 included four ratings for general programming—TV-G for all audiences; TV-PG for shows like "Baywatch" thought by their producers to contain "infrequent coarse language, limited violence, and some suggestive dialogue and situations"; TV-14 for those the networks thought contained "sophisticated themes, sexual content, strong language and more intense violence" such as "Cybill," "The Simpsons," or "Murder One"; and TV-M for those like "NYPD Blue" thought to be unsuitable for children under seventeen. In addition, there were two children's ratings, TV-Y indicating a show suitable for even the youngest children, and TV-Y7 for those recommended only for children over seven.

Such classifications were thought to be too vague and, because they were awarded by the networks themselves, too inconsistent. CBS rated "Late Night with David Letterman" as no more than a TV-PG while NBC thought "The Tonight Show with Jay Leno" merited a TV-14. Also, some shows like "Seinfeld" and "Homicide: Life on the Streets" could fluctuate from week to week, from TV-PG to TV-14 and back again. For this reason, the negotiators adopted in July 1997 a system which will tack on some additional letters to the existing age designations, as V for "intense violence," S for "intense sexual situations," L for "strong coarse language," and D for "intensely suggestive dialogue." To the children's categories there may be added an FV indicating "fantasy violence." Odd, that. Isn't all the violence on TV, bar that which the networks' journalistic arms are lucky enough to catch on the evening news, fantasy violence? . . .

RIDICULOUS ARGUMENTS

NBC has so far excluded itself from participation in the new scheme, introducing the idea of (in Walter Goodman's words) "worthwhile violence" in shows such as Schindler's List and "The Odyssey" and warning against the dangers of censorship from Washington at the behest of "radical" religious organizations. It will come as a surprise, perhaps, that this attitude has been taken up by the country's most profitable network, together with the "creative" people who supply them with their excellent product, with nothing but the noblest of motives. But it is not surprising at all that the press which covers the debate feels itself constrained by its own lofty pursuit of objectivity and balance from heaping upon such arguments the ridicule and contempt they deserve.

John Carmody in The Washington Post's "TV Column," for instance, reports on NBC's courting of the TV Writers Guild, assembled in Pasadena, California, in July 1997. Dick Wolf, producer of NBC's "Players" (a new comedy-drama for the 1997–

98 season), told the writers that the additional rating letters (NBC will continue to use the age-based system) were "absolutely coercion . . . and if you people don't think that this is a basic First Amendment issue, and truly frightening in its implications, you should do some homework.". . .

Speaking from an even more exalted position, also to the TV writers in Pasadena, was Warren Littlefield, president of NBC Entertainment:

> In my 20 years of broadcasting I have never been more afraid than I am of the content-rating issue . . . I've been afraid of a lot of things. This one is serious. It started, I think, as a little snowball that was rolling down the hill. And as broadcasters, I think we're looking at a potential avalanche right now. . . . It's no longer about a label. It's about controlling content.

Likewise, the network's president, Robert C. Wright, is quoted by Lawrie Mifflin in *The New York Times* as saying that the deal with the politicians and advocacy groups was a "slippery slope" down which his unfortunate competitors were sliding toward "censorship."

VIOLENCE AS ART

But a more subtle argument was used by Rosalyn P. Weinman, who has the title of executive vice president for broadcast standards at NBC. In an interview with Lawrie Mifflin and in an op-ed piece of her own in *The New York Times*, she cited the importance of context given to the sex and violence in such recent network offerings as *Schindler's List* and "The Odyssey"—and, she said, "context cannot be expressed in a rating letter."

> Parenting isn't simple. Neither is labeling television. In our quick-fix culture, the idea of just pressing a button to protect our children is seductive, but it won't work. In fact, the new labels can blur the distinction between high-quality television and programs with gratuitous sex and violence. For example, "The Odyssey," a TV movie based on Homer's epic that was broadcast last May [1997], would have carried a V rating, because it included some violent scenes, even though it was the kind of educational program parents want their children to watch. When the V-chip becomes reality, all shows with a specific rating could be indiscriminately blocked. . . .

> Like everyone else, interest groups and politicians have an important right to protest shows they don't like. But they shouldn't decide what people should see. And make no mistake, this new system is the first step by Congress toward suppressing certain kinds of shows.

Senator Joseph Lieberman of Connecticut has said the issue is not about "rating the garbage" but how to "get rid of the garbage."

When politicians decide to define what garbage is, all Americans have to live with their definition. This means fewer choices and programs that are less interesting, entertaining and provocative. And it could mean fewer programs that raise awareness for important issues, like domestic violence.

Talk about garbage! But Dr. Weinman gives the game away when she writes of "gratuitous sex and violence," relying on the now venerable argument that if the s and v are "artistically justified" then they're OK. The pop culture saw through this one a long time ago with its jokes about earnest young actresses agreeing to take their clothes off for men to ogle them so long as it is "artistically justified." The fact is, whatever may be the case with sex or violence in serious artistic media, everybody knows that they are always gratuitous on television.

"Happy Violence" on Television

In dramatic programs, violent scenes occur an average of 5 times per prime time and 20–25 times per Saturday morning program hour. They involve nearly half of all characters in prime-time, and more than 8 out of 10 characters in Saturday morning children's programs

Of course, there is blood in fairy tales, gore in mythology, murder in Shakespeare. But the individually crafted, historically-inspired, selectively used (and often dreadful) violence of art, folklore and journalism, capable of balancing tragic costs against deadly compulsions, has been swamped by "happy violence" produced for global sales on the dramatic assembly-line. Happy violence is swift, cool, painless, effective, and always leads to a happy ending. Marketing mayhem shuns tragedy and pain; it is designed to deliver an audience to the next commercial in an upbeat and receptive mood.

Much of the mayhem, especially in Saturday morning children's programs, is not only painless but also humorous. Humor is the sugar coating that makes the pill of cool, happy violence even more easily absorbed.

George Gerbner, *Media & Democracy: A Book of Readings and Resources*, 1996.

For instance, the networks are resisting the motion of the House of Representatives to bring back the "family hour" in the first hour of prime time because, as John Carmody put it, "the TV business is far more competitive than it was in the family hour's heyday, and . . . they must maintain their ability to appeal to the most attractive target audiences (read: viewers eighteen to thirty-four years old)." In other words, the networks know that it is *because* of their portrayal of sex and violence that people are tuning in. This makes the idea of setting serious and artistic representations of sex and violence against the merely "gratuitous" kind absurd. The so-called "context" of the serious shows is not, after all, the Holocaust (*Schindler's List*) or Greek legends ("The Odyssey") as Dr. Weinman pretends but *the TV context*, in which titillation is the name of the game, whether one is ostensibly showing programs with the seal of high-cultural approval or not.

Another version of the "context" argument, for example, came from John Wells, executive producer of "E.R.," who, according to Lawrie Mifflin,

> said he feared that the labels would cause many families to tar all similarly rated television shows with the same brush.

> "It will make it much more difficult to get a show like E.R. on the air," Mr. Wells said. "We have violence, but it's in the context of showing the terrible effects of violence—it's exactly the sort we should see. Violence is part of our society and as artists we are right to chronicle it"

This is even more laughable than Dr. Weinman's argument. Oh, so *that's* what you're doing, Mr. Barnum! How do people like this escape the ridicule that ought by rights to be heaped upon their heads for such disingenuous arguments? Notice that they never quite come right out and say what they prefer to assume, namely that television is in the business of disinterestedly producing high art, in which the question of gratuitous sex or violence might (or might not) be justified. This is because there is simply no escaping the fact that their network is selling a product to people who make no pretense of desiring an artistic experience but who simply want to be titillated.

THE BUSINESS OF TITILLATION

Neither "The Odyssey" nor *Schindler's List* nor any others among the tiny percentage of NBC's shows which might have some slight pretensions to artistic quality have to show sex or violence to achieve their presumably high-minded ends. Aeschylus and Sophocles managed quite well without having the violent acts themselves on the stage in Greek tragedy. But the commercial successes like "Seinfeld" or "E.R."—they *do* have to be suggestive or explicit in well-recognized ways because that is what people watch them for. It is as if you sat through *Schindler's List* (as perhaps some of the millions who watched it did) in order to catch a glimpse of somebody's naked backside. Only with NBC's run-of-the-mill product, the naked backside (figuratively speaking) is practically all there is.

That is why, for some years past, the prime-time sitcoms have vied with each other for such poor, as yet unused double-entendres as they can find, like hungry dogs fighting for scraps of offal in Senator Lieberman's garbage dump. For Dr. Weinman or Mr. Wells to pretend that their employers are engaged in an artistic enterprise and not in the business of titillating people for huge sums of money is simply ludicrous. For them to add that there would be dire consequences for the republic were they and their colleagues to make less huge sums of money by being restrained from certain sorts of titillation as broadcast over the public airwaves is not only ludicrous but vicious and dishonest as well. For there are a number of ways in which NBC stands to gain from refusing to go along with the agreement reached by the other networks. They will receive the gain in the reduced pressure for legislation while not having to pay the price in terms of putting off potential viewers. As Lawrie Mifflin noted, they could also gain "if producers decide to steer shows with adult themes to NBC because they know it will not be adding a V, S, L, or D label that could chase some viewers away."

VIEWS ON TELEVISION

All that having been said, I must add that I myself am skeptical about the usefulness of television "ratings" for sex and violence. There is certainly an argument to be made for leaving all the televisual garbage unraked and unburied so that its noisome stench will warn off parents who might otherwise think their children were coming to no harm through watching TV. As I have often said before, watching television is bad for children. Period. It is a myth and a chimera, subscribed to by guilt-ridden parents in need of the televisual baby sitter and connived at by the greedy TV industry that, if only the programming is of high enough quality, TV will stop being bad for children and start being good for them. It won't. Ever. Because at its best it is a wholly passive experience and it takes them away from those active ones, such as reading or playing games or practicing a musical instrument, from which alone they can learn something other than the sophisticated, prematurely knowing cynicism that TV produces.

But this is a hard saying for busy and indulgent parents in the late twentieth-century. They will continue, I predict, to prefer to believe that exactly calibrated government or industry regulation of the dangers their children face will allow them to continue to be uninvolved in raising them, or in instilling in them the moral will to resist those voyeuristic temptations which even the most socially conscious networks are in the business of dangling in front of them. Not for the first time, one of our big debates about "the media" will prove to have changed nothing of any importance.

| "A line has been crossed—not just of taste, but of human dignity and decency."

VIOLENT MOTION PICTURES DEBASE AMERICAN CULTURE

Robert Dole

Robert Dole served in the U.S. Senate from 1969 to 1996, when he resigned to run for president as the nominee of the Republican Party (Dole lost the election to Bill Clinton). The following viewpoint is taken from a May 31, 1995, speech that Dole delivered in Los Angeles, California, shortly after announcing his candidacy for the Republican presidential nomination. In the address, Dole attacks the American entertainment industry for putting profits ahead of human values by producing violent and degrading motion pictures and music recordings. He argues that such products threaten the nation's children and debase America's culture.

As you read, consider the following questions:

1. What two goals does Dole say he hopes to accomplish in his address?
2. What examples of media violence and depravity does Dole list?
3. How does Dole counter the argument that the entertainment industry is simply responding to a market demand for violent products?

Reprinted from "Trash Culture: Are Hollywood's Values Corrupting America's Young?" the *San Diego Union-Tribune*'s June 11, 1995, adaptation of a speech by Robert Dole, delivered May 31, 1995, in Los Angeles, by permission of Robert Dole.

It is time to talk about the future of America—about issues of moral importance, matters of social consequence.

During my announcement tour, I gave voice to concerns held across this country about what is happening to our popular culture. I made what I thought was an obvious point, a point that worries countless American parents: that one of the greatest threats to American family values is the way our popular culture ridicules them. Our music, movies, television and advertising regularly push the limits of decency, bombarding our children with destructive messages of casual violence and even more casual sex. And I concluded that we must hold Hollywood and the entire entertainment industry accountable for putting profit ahead of common decency.

THE ENTERTAINMENT INDUSTRY

So here I am in California—the home of the entertainment industry and to many of the people who shape our popular culture. And I'm asking for their help. I believe our country is crying out for leaders who will call us as a people to our better nature, not to profit from our weakness; who will bring back our confidence in the good, not play on our fears of life's dark corners. This is true for those of us who seek public office. And it is true for those who are blessed with the talent to lead America's vaunted entertainment industry.

Actors and producers, writers and directors, people of talent around the world dream of coming to Hollywood. Because if you are the best, this is where you are. Americans were pioneers in film and dominate worldwide today. The American entertainment industry is at the cutting edge of creative excellence, but also too often the leading edge of a culture becoming dangerously coarse.

I have two goals. One is to make crystal clear the effect this industry has on America's children, in the hope that it will rise to their defense. And the other is to speak more broadly to America about the corporate executives who hide behind the lofty language of free speech in order to profit from the debasing of America.

There is often heard in Hollywood a kind of "aw shucks" response to attempts to link cultural causes to societal effects. It's the "we just make movies people want" response. I'll take that up in a minute. But when they go to work tomorrow, when they sift through competing proposals for their time and their money, when they consider how badly they need the next job, I want the leaders of the entertainment industry to think about the influence they have on America's children.

CHILDREN AND THE MEDIA

Let there be no mistake; televisions and movie screens, boom-boxes and headsets are windows on the world for our children. If you are too old, or too sophisticated, or too close to the problem, just ask a parent. What to some is art, to our children is a nightly news report on the world outside their limited experience. What to some is make believe, to them is the "real skinny" on the adult world they are so eager to experience. Kids know firsthand what they see in their families, their schools, their immediate communities. But our popular culture shapes their view of the "real world." Our children believe those paintings in celluloid are reflections of reality. But I don't recognize America in much of what I see.

My voice and the rising voices of millions of other Americans who share this view represent more than the codgy old attempt of one generation to steal the fun of another. A line has been crossed—not just of taste, but of human dignity and decency. It is crossed every time sexual violence is given a catchy tune. When teen suicide is set to an appealing beat. When Hollywood's dream factories turn out nightmares of depravity.

You know what I mean. I mean *Natural Born Killers*. *True Romance*. Films that revel in mindless violence and loveless sex. I'm talking about groups like Cannibal Corpse, Geto Boys and 2 Live Crew. About a culture business that makes money from "music" extolling the pleasures of raping, torturing and mutilating women; from "songs" about killing policemen and rejecting law. The mainstreaming of deviancy must come to an end, but it will only stop when the leaders of the entertainment industry recognize and shoulder their responsibility.

Let me be clear: I am not saying that our growing social problems are entirely Hollywood's fault. They are not. People are responsible for their actions. Movies and music do not make children into murderers. But a numbing exposure to graphic violence and immorality does steal away innocence, smothering our instinct for outrage. We have reached the point where our popular culture threatens to undermine our character as a nation.

AMERICAN FREEDOMS

Which brings me to my second point. Our freedom is precious. I have risked my life to defend it, and would do so again. We must always be proud that in America we have the freedom to speak without Big Brother's permission.

Our freedom to reap the rewards of our capitalist system has raised the standard of living around the world. The profit motive is the engine of that system, and is honorable. But those who cultivate moral confusion for profit should understand this: we will name their names and shame them as they deserve to be shamed. We will contest them for the heart and soul of every child, in every neighborhood. For we who are outraged also have the freedom to speak. If we refuse to condemn evil, it is not tolerance but surrender. And we will never surrender.

Let me be specific. One of the companies on the leading edge of coarseness and violence is Time Warner. It is a symbol of how much we have lost. In the 1930s its corporate predecessor, Warner Brothers, made a series of movies, including *G-Men*, for the purpose of restoring "dignity and public confidence in the police." It made movies to help the war effort in the early 1940s. Its company slogan, put on a billboard across from the studio, was "Combining Good Citizenship With Good Picture Making."

Mike Ramirez. Reprinted by permission of Copley News Service.

Today Time Warner owns a company called Interscope Records which columnist John Leo called "the cultural equivalent of owning half the world's mustard gas factories." Ice-T of "Cop Killer" fame is one of Time Warner's "stars." I cannot bring myself to repeat the lyrics of some of the "music" Time Warner promotes. But our children do. There is a difference between the description of evil through art, and the marketing of evil through commerce. I would like to ask executives of Time Warner a question: Is this what you intended to accomplish with your careers? You have sold your souls, but must you debase our nation and threaten our children as well? [Editor's note: Time Warner has since sold its stake in Interscope and dropped Ice-T from its roster.]

Please do not answer that you are simply responding to the market. That is not true. In the movie business, as author Michael Medved points out, the most profitable films are the ones most friendly to the family. In 1994, the top five grossing films were the blockbusters *The Lion King*, *Forrest Gump*, *True Lies*, *The Santa Clause* and *The Flintstones*. To put it in perspective, it has been reported that *The Lion King* made six times as much money as *Natural Born Killers*.

A WIDESPREAD CONCERN

The corporate executives who dismiss my criticism should not misunderstand. Mine is not the objection of some tiny group of zealots or an ideological fringe. From inner city mothers to suburban mothers to families in rural America—parents are afraid, and growing angry. There once was a time when parents felt the community of adults was on their side. Now they feel surrounded by forces assaulting their children and their code of values.

This is not a partisan matter. I am a conservative Republican, but I am joined in this fight by moderates, independents and liberal Democrats. Sen. Bill Bradley has spoken eloquently on this subject, as has Sen. Paul Simon, who talks of our nation's "crisis of glamorized violence." And leaders of the entertainment industry are beginning to speak up, as well.

Mark Canton, the president of Universal Pictures, said, "Any smart businessperson can see what we must do—make some 'PG-rated films.' Together . . . we can make the needed changes. If we don't this decade will be noted in the history books as the embarrassing legacy of what began as a great art form. We will be labeled, 'the decline of an empire.'"

Change is possible—in Hollywood, and across the entertainment industry. There are few national priorities more urgent. I know that good and caring people work in this industry. If they are deaf to the concerns I have raised, it must be because they do not fully understand what is at stake. But we must make them understand. We must make it clear that tolerance does not mean neutrality between love and cruelty, between peace and violence, between right and wrong. Ours is not a crusade for censorship; it is a call for good citizenship.

When I announced I was running for president, I said that my mission is to rein in our government, to reconnect the powerful with the values which have made America strong and to reassert America's place as a great nation in the world. Tonight I am speaking beyond this room to some of the most powerful arbiters of our values. Tonight my challenge to the entertainment industry is to accept a calling above and beyond the bottom line—to fulfill a duty to the society which provides its profits. Help our nation maintain the innocence of its children. Prove to us that courage and conscience are alive and well in Hollywood.

"Horror films, like other violent fare,
can be culturally and artistically
significant."

A DEFENSE OF VIOLENT MOTION PICTURES

Craig Fischer

In several speeches during 1995 and 1996, Robert (Bob) Dole, then the Republican presidential candidate, castigated the entertainment industry for corrupting America's culture by producing violent and depraved movies. The following viewpoint is taken from Craig Fischer's open letter to Dole, written in response to these speeches. Fischer maintains that Dole's attacks are simplistic and misguided. Not all violent motion pictures are the same, he argues, and the way people respond to such movies depends on a complex combination of personal factors, including the viewer's background and biases. Furthermore, Fischer states that it is unlikely that a direct connection exists between media violence and the moral well-being of Americans. As a form of expression, violent entertainment has its place in a free American society, he concludes. At the time that this viewpoint was written, Fischer taught English at the University of Illinois in Urbana-Champaign. He is now a professor of English at Appalachian State University in North Carolina. Fischer is also an editor of *Cinema Journal*.

As you read, consider the following questions:

1. What admissions does Fischer make concerning his political leanings and taste in motion pictures?
2. What has academic film scholarship contributed to the debate over media violence, in the author's view?
3. How might the setting in which films are presented affect how viewers respond to them, according to Fischer?

Reprinted from Craig Fischer, "Trapped in the Web: An Open Letter to Bob Dole," *Images*, no. 1, August 1996, by permission of the author and *Images*.

D ear Bob:
      Let's be blunt: your 1996 Presidential campaign is off to
a fizzle of a start. . . . I suspect you'll be addressing some hot-
button issues—including media violence—in an attempt to
bring some much-needed zip to your campaign.

You've spoke out against media sex and violence before, even
as you've handled the issue inconsistently. I remember your
scathing condemnation of *Money Train* after the copycat firebombing of a New York subway ticket booth; I also recall your en-
dorsement of *True Lies* as a family film, despite its infidelity plot
and shots of Jamie Lee Curtis in lingerie licking a bed post.
(How much *does* Arnold Schwarzenegger donate to the party?)
But you usually denounce popular culture's "destructive messages of casual violence and even more casual sex," as in a
speech you gave in Los Angeles, the belly of the beast, on May
31, 1995:

> A line has been crossed—not just of taste, but of human dignity
> and decency. It is crossed every time sexual violence is given a
> catchy tune. When teen suicide is set to an appalling beat. When
> Hollywood's dream factories turn out nightmares of depravity.
> You know what I mean. I mean *Natural Born Killers*. *True Romance*.
> Films that revel in mindless violence and loveless sex.

And later in the speech you note that "a numbing exposure to
graphic violence and immorality does steal away innocence,
smothering our instinct for outrage. And I think we have reached
the point where our popular culture threatens to undermine our
character as a nation." But I don't buy your connection between
media "violence and immorality" and a weakened American
"character," and I hope you'll read on as I voice my objections.

ENJOYING VIOLENT MOVIES

Unlike you, Bob, I enjoy some violent movies. I'm not too crazy
about hoax documentaries like the *Faces of Death* series or *Snuff*,
because their low production values make them seem gritty and
real. But I love Hong Kong action films like *Hard Boiled*, a movie
whose climax, a prolonged gun battle in a hospital where patients are mowed down like dry grass, makes me laugh and
laugh. And I have a ball with American films—like *From Beyond*,
Evil Dead II and *Reservoir Dogs*—that traffic in similar over-the-top
aesthetics.

  As I watched *Re-animator* for the first time and marveled at the
sight of a severed head giving oral sex to a woman strapped to a
morgue table, I realized that I absolutely adore movies that spill
over the bounds of good taste.

My fascination with these movies is a little disturbing—what drive in my unconscious do these films speak to, anyway?—but I haven't yet felt the need to cut anyone's ear off.

I have an even more shocking confession to make, Bob. I'm liberal, I teach college, and my politics inform my teaching. Now I understand that putting "liberal" and "teach college" in the same sentence is enough to make a staunch Republican like yourself foam at the mouth.

VIOLENCE IN MOTION PICTURES

A motion picture is a fantasy, not real life. In the dark, we are hoodwinked and charmed into believing that the lives (and deaths) of the people in front of us—made-up people, ghosts, creations of the artist's imagination—actually have something to do with our own lives (and deaths) and actually, urgently matter.

But when the lights come up, the number of dead in the world has increased by a total of none, and the only thing that has been killed is your time (which, afterward, you will determine to be well or ill spent according to your own tastes)....

Do we tacitly endorse what we witness? The Greeks didn't think so. They believed that violence in art and violence in life are two different things altogether, and that while violence in life is destructive, violence in art need not be; that art provides a healthy channel for the natural aggressive forces within us, a safety valve, if you will.

Hal Hinson, *Washington Post*, May 23, 1993.

Surely I must be part of that cabal of "tenured radicals" who brainwash our kids into accepting the evils of premarital sex, abortion and water fluoridation. Well, not quite; I don't have a tenure-track job, I'm not paid very well, and I haven't the faintest idea how to hypnotize my students into believing what I believe. Conservative education critics rely on a "Monkey see, monkey do" theory to explain the relationship between a teacher and his/her students . . . which, come to think of it, is mighty close to your own theories about the effects of movie violence, Bob. But the theory crumbles like cardboard when we understand that our students are people, with enough intelligence and independence to evaluate facts, argue points, and make up their own minds about important issues.

In my classes, I've taught *I've Heard the Mermaids Singing*, *Do the Right Thing*, *Daughters of the Dust*, and *Go Fish* because these movies deal with topics—radical politics, African American history, gay and lesbian culture—that Hollywood cinema usually marginal-izes or ignores. These movies also provoke spirited discussions; the students aren't shy about expressing their opinions about the issues these films raise, even if their opinions are opposed to mine. And I'm happy to teach these films because I *like* them as much as Jackie Chan Kung-Fu fights and Fred Williamson blax-ploitation pics.

A SEEMING CONTRADICTION

Now, Bob, you may see a contradiction here. How is it possible for me to support liberalism and teach feminist films while I enjoy horror films where women get cunnilingized by severed heads?

Well, I think that *all* spectators experience similar forms of cognitive dissonance, because we're all caught in a complex web of relationships that exerts a profound effect on our media re-ception. Some strands of the web are woven from our own de-sires and pleasures; others are woven by the particular TV show or film we're watching; still others are woven by ideological and social forces.

Because of this web, the act of watching a film (even a gory, drippy, bloody one) involves complicated layers of reasoning and response that can't be simplified into a campaign sound bite. . . .

ACADEMIC FILM CRITICISM

In my . . . attempts to figure out my affection for violent films, . . . I found some answers in current academic film history. . . .

This new historical scholarship combines factual research and interpretive theory in accessible and enlightening ways. By look-ing closely at the interactions between media texts, spectators, and historical and ideological contexts, critics like David Bord-well, Janet Staiger, Henry Jenkins, Richard Dyer, Lea Jacobs, Tom Doherty and others offer useful frameworks for understanding how films (and, by extension, other types of media) affect audi-ences. The new historians' areas of emphasis—text, spectator, context—quite nicely address the issue of violence:

• *What role do individual films and TV programs play in influencing specta-tor reactions?* You talk as if all violent films are the same, Bob, but that's ridiculous. I can identify a truckload of contemporary horror movies, for instance, that do a lot more than just serve up steaming viscera. What about the broadsides against con-sumerism in *Dawn of the Dead*, or the trenchant critiques of the media in *Piranha* and *The Howling*? (Robin Wood makes some sharp observations about the contemporary horror film in *Holly-*

wood from Vietnam to Reagan.) Horror films, like other violent fare, can be culturally and artistically significant; evaluations like this need to be made on a film-to-film basis, person-to-person basis, and not through a simplistic denunciation of all media violence.

• *Where do spectators fit into all this?* Bob, the automatic connection you draw between media and real-life mayhem ignores the complexity and subjective nature of audience-film relationships. Why do you watch a TV show or movie? To see exploding cars and other property damage? To escape the work-a-day grind? To dream about attractive stars? To catalog the newest entry in a beloved genre? To watch cool special effects? To encounter the personal vision of the auteur(s) responsible for the film? Chances are your reasons are an unruly mixture of these and a hundred more, some of which reflect your personal desires and others that you've picked up from your family, education, and exposure to other media. Janet Staiger calls these preferences *reading strategies*, and argues that individual spectators often exercise contradictory reading strategies while watching a film. As Staiger writes, "As a student of Hollywood cinema, I find *Raiders of the Lost Ark* a masterpiece of filmmaking, but as a feminist I am appalled." I teach feminist films while I admire the aestheticism of the murder-by-stabbing-and-hanging at the beginning of *Suspiria*.

• *What is the role of environment in audience response?* It seems like common sense to claim that where and how you saw a movie affects your reception. These effects are sometimes pretty prosaic; maybe you hated seeing *Batman* at the multiplex because a guy behind you kept loudly rustling his popcorn bag, but this has nothing to do with the film. But what if you saw *Halloween* as part of a college course on gender and contemporary film? Or what if you watched *Bloodsucking Freaks* in a sticky-floor grindhouse with a male audience that exhibited undue relish over the film's numerous killing scenes? Do teenage kids take horror films seriously, or do they establish a healthy distance between themselves and movies like *Freddy's Dead: The Final Nightmare*? Do films like *Natural Born Killers* have more violent power on the big screen or on video? These are significant questions, and Jeff Sconce, Carol Clover, Tim Corrigan, and other critics have taken the first steps towards answering them. Check out what they say before you make the "violent film" issue a big theme of your campaign, Bob.

ALL EFFECTS ARE LOCAL

As far as I'm concerned, this complex web of film, spectator and context makes all responses to texts as sloppy, complicated, and contradictory as my own to violent movies. This sloppiness invalidates your one-on-one correlation between visual and audience effects, Bob, and it also defines the study of media effects as a troublingly inexact endeavor. I don't believe we can ever adequately understand media effects on audiences, since response depends so heavily on the subjectivities of each individual spectator, who—due to race, class, gender, intellectual training, conditions of reception, notions of pleasure, and a thousand other personal factors—may or may not be predisposed to consider a film or TV show "good" or "bad," or "capable of riling up a postal worker enough to go out and open fire at McDonalds." All media effects are local, and a reliable model of audience response should acknowledge that a number of responses (perhaps an infinite number) are possible to any artwork in a given historical moment.

This *doesn't* mean, however, that spectator interpretation is a model democracy or a perfectly level playing field. The idea of "bounded interpretation"—as forwarded by Staiger, Richard Dyer, and other scholars—makes some sensible points about the question of media influence. As Dyer writes,

> We are all restricted by both the viewing and the reading codes
> to which we have access (by virtue of where we are situated in
> the world and the social order) and by what representations
> there are for us to view and read. The prestige of high culture,
> the centralization of mass cultural production, the literal poverty
> of marginal cultural production: these are aspects of the power
> relations of representation that put the weight of the control
> over representation on the side of the rich, the white, the male,
> the heterosexual.

In other words: rich, white, straight guys (your homeys, Bob!) run the media, and thus have an inordinate power in determining reading strategies. But as Staiger reminds us, these elites haven't fully colonized the subconscious of the mass audience; smaller, more subversive reading strategies percolate beneath the orthodoxy of mass opinion, occasionally surfacing as weird rumors, conspiracy theories or downright insurrection. Even though certain reading strategies and subject positions are dominant in any given historical moment, there's always the possibility for oppositional positions, too. And all these different ways of looking at TV shows, watching movies, and listening to CDs lead to multiple responses and effects.

No Easy Generalities

So I think you're way off-base, Bob, in your assumption that the wanton sex and violence portrayed in the media is debasing our nation and threatening our children. The situation is just too complex to fit into easy generalities. You and me and everybody else, we're all figuring out *personal* answers about how we've been influenced by the media. I'll keep trying to understand my attraction to violent movies as long as you promise not to censor culture in defense of the American "character," deal? I can't help but think that the mingling of multiple reading strategies with various forms of violent and non-violent entertainment creates a productive chaos, a multifaceted society where all viewpoints receive an airing and none are suppressed. A utopia it ain't, but home it is.

PERIODICAL BIBLIOGRAPHY

The following articles have been selected to supplement the diverse views presented in this chapter. Addresses are provided for periodicals not indexed in the *Readers' Guide to Periodical Literature*, the *Alternative Press Index*, the *Social Sciences Index*, or the *Index to Legal Periodicals and Books*.

Philip Berroll — "Cultural Elites, Closet Values," *Tikkun*, September/October 1993.

Margaret Carlson — "Dole: The Movie, Part II," *Time*, August 12, 1996.

Thomas Fleming — "In Praise of Sex and Violence," *Chronicles*, July 1994. Available from 928 N. Main St., Rockford, IL 61103.

George Gilder — "Overthrowing Hollywood and the Broadcast Elites," *New Perspectives Quarterly*, Spring 1995.

John D. Hagen Jr. — "It's Time to Take Sides: Catholicism, Yes; Popular Culture, No," *Commonweal*, September 22, 1995.

Irving Kristol — "Children, Hollywood, and Censorship," *American Enterprise*, September/October 1995.

Dave Marsh — "Cops 'n' Gangstas," *Nation*, June 26, 1995.

Michael Medved — "Hollywood's Three Big Lies," *Reader's Digest*, October 1995.

Frank Rich — "Double Agents in Our Culture Wars," *New York Times*, December 14, 1995.

Tricia Rose — "Rap Music and the Demonization of Young Black Males," *USA Today*, May 1994.

Richard Schickel — "No, but He Reads the Polls," *Time*, June 12, 1995.

Brian Siano — "Frankenstein Must Be Destroyed: Chasing the Monster of TV Violence," *Humanist*, January/February 1994.

John P. Sisk — "The Poetry of Violence," *American Scholar*, Spring 1997.

Oliver Stone — "The David Letterman Disease," *New Perspectives Quarterly*, Spring 1995.

David Thomson — "A Gore Phobia," *Esquire*, May 1997.

Richard Zoglin — "A Company Under Fire," *Time*, June 12, 1995.

FOR FURTHER DISCUSSION

CHAPTER 1

1. The authors of the National Television Violence Study assert that it is important to examine the context in which violence occurs. Does John Leo agree that context is important? If so, what is the source of his disagreements with the NTVS's conclusions regarding the seriousness and prevalence of television violence? Explain.

2. Madeline Levine claims that "the debate is over" on whether media violence harms children. Jonathan Freedman considers the evidence of the harmful effects of media violence to be "laughable." Jon Katz calls the idea that media violence induces mayhem "idiotic." In your opinion, do such sweeping and strong descriptors strengthen or weaken the authors' general arguments? Explain your answer.

3. Jonathan Freedman argues that many researchers of media violence are predisposed to disfavor television violence. Does he provide evidence to support his claim? Can evidence of such bias be found in the viewpoints of John P. Murray or Madeline Levine? Explain your answer.

4. James K. Fitzpatrick uses his personal experience as a high school teacher to support his view that music causes little lasting harm for most students. How effective is this tactic? Are his comments concerning teenagers congruent with your own observations? Explain.

CHAPTER 2

1. Helen K. Liebowitz argues that although she and the National Parent-Teachers Association oppose government censorship, they believe steps must be taken to reduce media violence. Is there a contradiction in this position? If so, does Liebowitz successfully resolve it in her arguments? Can society restrict media violence without resorting to censorship, according to Liebowitz? According to the American Civil Liberties Union? Explain your answer, citing examples from the viewpoints.

2. The ACLU maintains that limits on television violence could only be warranted if there existed a "clear cause-and-effect relationship between what normal children see on TV and harmful actions." In your judgment, should the reason to support restrictions on media violence be stated more broadly or narrowly? For instance, if media violence can be demonstrated to be just one of several causes of violence, or if a rela-

tionship between media and real-life violence cannot be proven with 100 percent certainty, could restrictions on television violence still be appropriate? Or should censorship be avoided in all circumstances? Explain your answer.

3. Solveig Bernstein argues that the V-chip and the way the government is mandating its use constitutes government censorship of television, while Dick Rolfe and Edward Markey disagree. What arguments does each person make to support his or her respective position? Which argument do you find the strongest? Why?

CHAPTER 3

1. Are the suggestions of the National Crime Prevention Council and Madeline Levine mutually exclusive? Could parents implement both strategies? Explain.

2. Does Chiori Santiago's personal and informal writing style strengthen or weaken her arguments, in your opinion? Explain, giving examples from the viewpoint. Would you be willing to live without television for a week or more? Why or why not?

3. What "straw man" argument of the media industry does Joseph Lieberman attempt to refute? What point is he trying to make about the influence of the media in society? Do you agree with his analysis? Why or why not?

4. According to Elizabeth Thoman, what "wrong" question has the media violence debate been focused on? Do you agree or disagree with her view that this question limits the debate on media violence in a counterproductive way? Explain.

CHAPTER 4

1. Why is the televised violence of sports and TV news ignored while violent fictional shows are condemned, according to David Link? In the author's opinion, what important element or elements does fictional violence possess that nonfiction news does not? Do you agree or disagree with his analysis? Why?

2. What word would you use to characterize the general tenor of James Bowman's article? Serious? Sarcastic? Frivolous? Angry? Does the article's tone add to or detract from the persuasiveness of Bowman's arguments? Explain, using passages from the viewpoint.

3. Both Link and Bowman compare contemporary media violence with the often violent plays of the ancient Greeks. What similarities or differences does each author point out in making his comparison? Which author do you believe makes his argument more effectively? Explain.

4. Craig Fischer gives one particular perspective of the political context in which Bob Dole made his attack on Hollywood motion pictures. In your opinion, is the fact that Dole was running for president at the time a relevant factor in analyzing his arguments? Why or why not?

5. Of the motion pictures that Bob Dole and Craig Fischer mentioned in their viewpoints, which, if any, have you personally seen? Try to remember how the films affected you. Does your experience in watching these movies correspond more with Dole's arguments or with Fischer's? Explain your answer.

ORGANIZATIONS TO CONTACT

The editors have compiled the following list of organizations concerned with the issues debated in this book. The descriptions are derived from materials provided by the organizations. All have publications or information available for interested readers. The list was compiled on the date of publication of the present volume; the information provided here may change. Be aware that many organizations take several weeks or longer to respond to inquiries, so allow as much time as possible.

American Civil Liberties Union (ACLU)
125 Broad St., 18th Fl., New York, NY 10004-2400
(212) 549-2500
e-mail: aclu@aclu.org • web address: http://www.aclu.org

The ACLU champions the rights set forth in the Declaration of Independence and the Constitution. It opposes the censoring of any form of speech, including media depictions of violence. The ACLU publishes the quarterly newsletter *Civil Liberties Alert* and several handbooks, project reports, civil liberties books, pamphlets, and public policy reports, including *ACLU Expresses Concerns on TV Rating Scheme: Says "Voluntary" System is Government-Backed Censorship.*

American Psychological Association (APA)
Office of Public Affairs
750 First St. NE, Washington, DC 20002-4242
(202) 336-5700
e-mail: public.affairs@apa.org • web address: http://www.apa.org

This society of psychologists aims to "advance psychology as a science, as a profession, and as a means of promoting human welfare." Although it believes that viewing television violence can have potential dangers for children, it opposes the creation of an age-based television ratings system. APA produces numerous publications, including *Children and Television Violence* and *APA Denounces Proposed Age-Based Television Rating System.*

Canadians Concerned About Violence in Entertainment (C-CAVE)
167 Glen Rd., Toronto, ON M4W 2W8, CANADA
(416) 961-0853 • fax: (416) 929-2720

C-CAVE works to increase public awareness about the effects of entertainment violence on society. It serves as an educational resource center by collecting and making available information about violence in entertainment. C-CAVE promotes media literacy and responsible government and industry regulation of media violence as essential ways to achieve a safer, healthier environment. C-CAVE publishes various newsletters, reports, and brochures concerning entertainment violence.

Cato Institute

1000 Massachusetts Ave. NW, Washington, DC 20001

(202) 842-0200 • fax: (202) 842-3490

e-mail: cato@cato.org • web address: http://www.cato.org

The institute is a libertarian public policy research foundation dedicated to promoting limited government, individual political liberty, and free-market economics. It opposes government regulation of television violence and the installation of the V-chip. It publishes the bimonthly *Policy Report* and the periodic *Cato Journal*.

Federal Communications Commission (FCC)

1919 M St. NW, Washington, DC 20554

(888) CallFCC (225-5322) • (202) 418-0200 • fax: (202) 418-0232

e-mail: fccinfo@fcc.gov • web address: http://www.fcc.gov

The FCC is an independent government agency responsible for regulating telecommunications. It develops and implements policy concerning interstate and international communications by radio, television, wire, satellite, and cable. The FCC is required to review the educational programming efforts of the networks. It publishes various reports, updates, and reviews that can be accessed on-line at their website.

Healing Our Nation from Violence

1300 Civic Dr., Suite 5, Walnut Creek, CA 94596

(510) 932-6943 • fax: (510) 932-1465

Healing Our Nation from Violence works to reduce entertainment industry violence and to connect adult mentors with low-income, at-risk youth. It supports the annual National TV-Turnoff Week and distributes the "Way More Fun Than TV" list to encourage people not to watch violent television programming. The organization believes that violence and anger can only be assuaged by creativity and service. It publishes various pamphlets, reports, and information sheets.

Media Coalition

139 Fulton St., Suite 302, New York, NY 10038

(212) 587-4025 • fax: (212) 587-2436

e-mail: mediacoalition@mediacoalition.org

web address: http://www.mediacoalition.org

The Media Coalition defends the First Amendment right to produce and sell books, magazines, recordings, videotapes, and video games. It defends the American public's right to have access to the broadest possible range of opinion and entertainment, including works considered offensive or harmful due to their violent or sexually explicit nature. It opposes the government-mandated ratings system for television. Media Coalition distributes to its members regular reports outlining the activities of Congress, state legislatures, and the courts on issues related to the First Amendment.

Mediascope
12711 Ventura Blvd., Suite 440, Studio City, CA 91604
(818) 508-2080 • fax: (818) 508-2088
e-mail: facts@mediascope.org
web address: http://www.mediascope.org

Mediascope is a nonprofit, public policy organization founded to promote constructive depictions of health and social issues in media. It provides tools and information to help the entertainment community be more socially responsible without relinquishing creative freedom. Mediascope publishes various issue briefs and articles, including *Media Violence Risk Factors* and *Media Ratings: Design, Use, and Consequences.*

MediaWatch
517 Wellington St. West, Suite 204, Toronto, ON M5V 1G1, CANADA
(416) 408-2065 • fax: (416) 408-2069
e-mail: mediawatch@myna.com
web address: http://www.myna.com/~mediawat

MediaWatch is a feminist organization that works to improve the portrayal of women and girls in the media. It believes the media perpetuate the image of women as sexual objects, which contributes to a society where violence against women is tolerated. It publishes the newsletter *Bulletin* three times per year as well as various guides to help people write clear and concise letters to government officials in order to promote the campaign for gender equality.

National Cable Television Association (NCTA)
1724 Massachusetts Ave. NW, Washington, DC 20036-1969
(202) 775-3550 • fax: (202) 775-3675
web address: http://www.ncta.com

NCTA is the cable industry's major trade association. Its primary goal is to provide a single, unified voice on issues affecting the cable industry. NCTA works to advance the public policies of the cable television industry before Congress, the executive branch, the courts, and the American public. It publishes various reports and news releases that can be accessed at its website.

National Coalition on Television Violence (NCTV)
5132 Newport Ave., Bethesda, MD 20816
e-mail: reach@nctvv.org • web address: http://www.nctvv.org

NCTV is a research and education association dedicated to reducing the violence in films and television programming. It distributes ratings, reviews, and violence research. It publishes the quarterly *NCTV News* as well as various reports and educational materials.

National PTA
330 N. Wabash Ave., Suite 2100, Chicago, IL 60611-3690
(312) 670-6782
e-mail: info@pta.org • web address: http://www.pta.org

The National PTA is the oldest and largest child advocacy organization in the United States. It opposed the original age-based television rating system and worked with the television industry and other child advocates to develop the age plus content-based rating system that went into effect in 1997. The National PTA produces *Our Children* magazine, various surveys, reports, and on-line bulletins on issues related to the health, welfare, and education of children and youth.

Parents Television Council (PTC)
PO Box 712067, Los Angeles, CA 90071-9934
(213) 621-2506
e-mail: parentstv@compuserve.com
web address: http://www.ParentsTV.org

PTC was established as a special project of the Media Research Center. Its goal is to bring America's demand for values-driven television programming to the entertainment industry. PTC produces an annual *Family Guide to Prime Time Television*, based on scientific monitoring and analysis generated from the Media Research Center's computerized Media Tracking System. The *Family Guide* profiles every sitcom and drama on the major television networks and provides information on subject matter that is inappropriate for children. PTC also publishes various reports, including *A Vanishing Haven: The Decline of the Family Hour*.

TV-FreeAmerica
1611 Connecticut Ave. NW, Suite 3A, Washington, DC 20009
(202) 887-0436 • fax: (202) 518-5560
e-mail: tvfa@essential.org • web address: http://www.tvfa.org

TV-FreeAmerica is a national nonprofit organization that encourages Americans to reduce the amount of television they watch in order to promote stronger families and communities. It sponsors the National TV-Turnoff Week, when more than 5 million people across the country go without television for seven days. It publishes the quarterly newsletter the *TV-Free American*.

The UNESCO International Clearinghouse
on Children and Violence on the Screen
Nordicom, Goteborg University, Box 713, 405 30 Goteborg, Sweden
e-mail: feilitzen@jmk.su.se • web address: http://www.nordicom.gu.se

The clearinghouse disseminates information about the relationship between young people and media violence, alternatives to media violence, and efforts to reduce violence in the media. It publishes a yearbook and a newsletter three times per year.

BIBLIOGRAPHY OF BOOKS

Charles R. Acland — *Youth, Murder, Spectacle: The Cultural Politics of "Youth in Crisis."* Boulder, CO: Westview Press, 1995.

Martin Barker and Julian Petley, eds. — *Ill Effects: The Media-Violence Debate.* New York: Routledge, 1997.

Steven J. Bennett — *Kick the TV Habit: A Simple Program for Changing Your Family's Television Viewing and Video Game Habits.* New York: Penguin, 1994.

David Bianculli — *Teleliteracy: Taking Television Seriously.* New York: Continuum, 1994.

Sissela Bok — *Mayhem: Violence as Public Entertainment.* Reading, MA: Addison-Wesley, 1998.

Laurent Bouzereau — *Ultraviolent Movies: From Sam Peckinpah to Quentin Tarantino.* Secaucus, NJ: Carol, 1996.

Peter Brooker and Will Brooker, eds. — *Postmodern After-images: A Reader in Film, Television, and Video.* New York: Edward Arnold, 1997.

Milton Chen — *The Smart Parent's Guide to Kids' TV.* San Francisco: KQED Books, 1994.

Robert Coles — *The Moral Intelligence of Children.* New York: Random House, 1997.

George Comstock — *Television and the American Child.* San Diego: Academic Press, 1991.

Cynthia A. Cooper — *Violence on Television: Congressional Inquiry, Public Criticism, and Industry Response: A Policy Analysis.* Lanham, MD: University Press of America, 1996.

Renee R. Curry and Terry L. Allison, eds. — *States of Rage: Emotional Eruption, Violence, and Social Change.* New York: New York University Press, 1996.

Kathy Edgar — *Everything You Need to Know About Media Violence.* New York: Rosen, 1998.

Gary R. Edgerton, Michael T. Marsden, and Jack Nachbar, eds. — *In the Eye of the Beholder: Critical Perspectives in Popular Film and Television.* Bowling Green, OH: Bowling Green State University, 1997.

Herbert N. Foerstel — *Banned in the Media: A Reference Guide to Censorship in the Press, Motion Pictures, Broadcasting, and the Internet.* Westport, CT: Greenwood, 1998.

Jib Fowles — *Why Viewers Watch: A Reappraisal of Television's Effects.* Newbury Park, CA: Sage, 1992.

Gregory Giagnocavo and Vince Distefano, eds. — *Child Safety on the Internet.* Upper Saddle River, NJ: Prentice Hall Computer Books, 1997.

Jeffrey H. Goldstein, ed.	*Why We Watch: The Attractions of Violent Entertainment.* New York: Oxford University Press, 1998.
Dave Grossman	*On Killing: The Psychological Cost of Learning to Kill in War and Society.* Boston: Little, Brown, 1995.
Barbara Hattemer and Robert Showers	*Don't Touch That Dial: The Impact of the Media on Children and the Family.* Lafayette, LA: Huntington House, 1993.
Stephen Hunter	*Violent Screen: A Critic's Thirteen Years on the Front Lines of Movie Mayhem.* Baltimore: Bancroft Press, 1995.
Aletha C. Huston et al.	*Big World, Small Screen: The Role of Television in American Society.* Lincoln: University of Nebraska Press, 1992.
P.T. Kelly, ed.	*Television Violence: A Guide to the Literature.* New York: Nova Science, 1996.
Bakari Kitwana	*The Rap on Gangsta Rap: Who Run It?: Gangsta Rap and Visions of Black Violence.* Chicago: Third World Press, 1994.
John Leonard	*Smoke and Mirrors: Violence, Television, and Other American Cultures.* New York: New Press, 1997.
Diane E. Levin	*Teaching Young Children in Violent Times: Building a Peaceable Classroom.* Cambridge, MA: Educators for Social Responsibility, 1994.
Madeline Levine	*Viewing Violence: How Media Violence Affects Your Child's and Adolescent's Development.* New York: Doubleday, 1996.
Jack Livesley and Frank Trotz	*The Penguin Guide to Children's TV and Video.* Toronto, Ontario: Penguin, 1993.
Tannis M. MacBeth, ed.	*Tuning In to Young Viewers: Social Science Perspectives on Television.* Thousand Oaks, CA: Sage, 1996.
Mike Males	*The Scapegoat Generation: America's War on Adolescents.* Monroe, ME: Common Courage Press, 1996.
Newton N. Minow and Craig L. Lamay	*Abandoned in the Wasteland: Children, Television, and the First Amendment.* New York: Hill and Wang, 1995.
David E. Newton	*Violence and the Media: A Reference Handbook.* Santa Barbara, CA: ABC-CLIO, 1996.
William Eric Perkins, ed.	*Droppin' Science: Critical Essays on Rap Music and Hip Hop Culture.* Philadelphia: Temple University Press, 1996.
Ronin Ro	*Gangsta: Merchandizing the Rhymes of Violence.* New York: St. Martin's Press, 1996.
Barry Sanders	*A is for Ox: Violence, Electronic Media, and the Silencing of the Written Word.* New York: Pantheon Books, 1994.

Kevin W. Saunders	*Violence as Obscenity: Limiting the Media's First Amendment Protection.* Durham, NC: Duke University Press, 1996.
Victoria Sherrow	*Violence and the Media: The Question of Cause and Effect.* Brookfield, CT: Millbrook Press, 1996.
David Allen Walsh	*Selling Out America's Children: How America Puts Profits Before Values—and What Parents Can Do.* Minneapolis: Fairview Press, 1995.
Franklin E. Zimring and Gordon Hawkins	*Crime Is Not the Problem: Lethal Violence in America.* New York: Oxford University Press, 1997.

INDEX